Searching for Truth

COMPILED AND EDITED BY

Cheryl Price, Ph.D.

Evangeline Carey, M.A.

Rosa Sailes, Ed.D.

Urban Ministries, Inc.

URBAN MINISTRIES, INC.
CHICAGO, ILLINOIS

Urban Ministries, Inc.

UMI (Urban Ministries, Inc.)
P. O. Box 436987
Chicago, Illinois 60643-6987
1-800-860-8642
www.urbanministries.com

First Edition
First Printing

Scripture quotations marked KJV, or unmarked, are from the King James Version.

Scripture quotations marked NIV are taken from the HOLY BIBLE, NEW INTERNATIONAL VERSION®, copyright © 1973, 1978, 1984 Biblica. Used by permission of Zondervan. All rights reserved.

Scripture quotations marked NLT are taken from the Holy Bible, New Living Translation, copyright © 1996, 2004. Used by permission of Tyndale House Publishers, Inc., Wheaton, Illinois 60189. All rights reserved.

Scripture quotations marked NASB are taken from the NEW AMERICAN STANDARD BIBLE®, Copyright © 1960, 1962, 1963, 1968, 1971, 1972, 1973, 1975, 1977, 1995 by The Lockman Foundation. Used by permission.

Searching for Truth has been compiled and edited by
Cheryl Price, Ph.D.; Evangeline Carey, M.A.; and Rosa Sailes, Ed.D.

Library of Congress Cataloguing in Publication Data
ISBN-10: 1609970012
ISBN-13: 9781609970017
1. Christian living 2. African American

Library of Congress Control Number: 2010937173

Printed in the United States of America.

Cover Design and Layout
Verve Marketing Group.

Dedication

WE DEDICATE THIS BOOK TO THOSE WHO
SEEK AND EMBRACE THE TRUTH OF JESUS.
THANK YOU TO OUR UMI TEAM FOR
THEIR HARD WORK AND DEDICATION.

Contents

    *Recommended for five-day VBS course

Introduction

PEARLS OF
SPIRITUAL TRUTH

The parables of Jesus can be thought of as pearls of spiritual truth for us. The stories and illustrations that Jesus gives in the parables continue to beckon us to search deeper and expand our hearts, minds, ears, and eyes to experience Christ beyond our initial encounter with Him. Like a pearl that is nestled inside of an oyster that we must open in order to receive the precious gem, we too must open up ourselves to see and receive what Jesus says through the parables.

To help us better understand the parables spoken by Jesus, we will begin with the defining thoughts of a parable. Commonly, a parable is the comparison of circumstances or objects in nature or in human experiences to illustrate a spiritual meaning—a spiritual truth. For example, in the parable of the mustard seed (Matthew 13:31–32), Jesus used an object found in nature, a mustard seed, to compare to the kingdom of heaven. Another way to understand a parable is to compare what is "known (mustard seed) with what is unknown (the kingdom of heaven)" (Cully, 1990).

As we search and discover the truth from Jesus through the parables, we need to remind ourselves that there may be more than one point or interpretation in Jesus' stories or illustrations. To stay focused, remember that "a good basic rule in interpreting parables is to look for the one main point of the parable, and be wary of other points that are brought out of it" ("Participatory Bible Study: Interpreting Parables").

The Gospels record 57 parables of Jesus. This accounts for one-third of the sayings from Jesus found in the Bible. Jesus' use of parables was obviously a regular form of communicating the truth about the kingdom of heaven and other godly principles. Jesus' regular use of parables was noted by the disciples. They asked Jesus why He spoke in parables. Although these stories seemed simple to grasp, the people gathering and following Jesus from place to place often could not understand the parables. They had hardened hearts, their ears were not open to hear, and their eyes were blind to Jesus, as recorded in Matthew 13:15–16 (KJV):

"For this people's heart is waxed gross, and their ears are dull of hearing, and their eyes they have closed; lest at any time they should see with their eyes and hear with their ears, and should understand with their heart, and should be converted, and I should heal them. But blessed are your [the disciples'] eyes, for they see: and your ears, for they hear."

Although it has been thousands of years since Jesus spoke the parables to the first century Church, His words and meanings conveyed through these stories continue to resonate with us today. We can see that each parable has its own hidden meaning that we are to hear and see for ourselves through Jesus. Like many of the ancient biblical people, we must not let our stubbornness, blindness, and unwillingness to hear Jesus keep us from accepting Him and following Him.

We invite each of you to learn more about parables and how we can respond to Jesus as you read *Searching for Truth*. In *Searching for Truth*, we have selected 10 parables for you to read, actively participate in, and receive your precious pearls as you learn more about or revisit what Jesus was saying through the parables. The 10 parables are from the Gospels of Matthew, Mark, and Luke. Each biblical parable is connected to everyday life issues and spiritually related principles from the love of money, to care, to forgiveness. Our titles are:

1. The Wise Man and Foolish Man
2. The Unforgiving Servant
3. The Talents
4. The Sower

5. The Good Samaritan
6. The Rich Fool
7. The Prodigal Son
8. The Rich Man and Lazarus
9. The Persistent Widow
10. The Pharisee and the Tax Collector

Each of these parables challenges us to ask questions about our relationship to God and others. Some of the questions that we may ask ourselves or want to consider are: *(1) Does God want me to forgive every time? (2) What happens if I don't forgive? (3) Does it matter to God how I live? (4) When I pray, is God listening?* and *(5) Are there heavenly treasures for me?*

The truth in the parables of Jesus is nestled the imagery that Jesus shares from nature and life. To discover these truths, we must open up ourselves to new possibilities. We need to have a willingness to let our eyes and ears become uncovered and sharpened to know, accept, and live out the spiritual truth that Jesus shares with us in His Holy Word.

SOURCES

Cully, Kendrig and Iris Cully. *Encyclopedia of Religious Education.* San Francisco, CA: Harper & Row, 1990. 469.

"Participatory Bible Study: Interpreting Parables."Deep Bible Study.com. www.deepbiblestudy.com/interpret_parables.php (accessed July 4, 2010).

THE WISE MAN AND THE FOOLISH MAN

Based on Matthew 7:21–27

KEY VERSE ⌒

"NOT EVERY ONE THAT SAITH UNTO ME, LORD, LORD, SHALL ENTER INTO THE KINGDOM OF HEAVEN; BUT HE THAT DOETH THE WILL OF MY FATHER WHICH IS IN HEAVEN"

(Matthew 7:21, KJV).

OPENING PRAYER ⌒

Lord, thank You for Your Word which is rich in wisdom and knowledge, and for Your Holy Spirit who empowers believers to follow You faithfully. Help me to honor Your presence in my life with obedience to Your words without compromise.

WORDS TO CONSIDER ⌒

1. KINGDOM OF HEAVEN (Matthew 7:21). A reference to God's order for the world; also a reference to heaven or eternal life with God.

2. LORD (vv. 21, 22). A reference to God.

3. PROPHESIED (v. 22). To speak the words of God or to speak about future events.

4. INIQUITY (v. 23). Sin.

5. GOD'S WILL (v. 21). That which God expects us to do.

INTRODUCTION ⌒

In the Old Testament, the books of Job, Proverbs, and Ecclesiastes are known as the books of "Wisdom Literature."

Throughout history, parables have been among the styles of expression used to impart knowledge to the young and the naïve. In ancient cultures, the use of parables and analogies was the equivalent of a textbook and served as an instructional delivery method to teach thinking and leadership skills to the next generation of rulers and elite young men. In the oral tradition in Africa, as well as the pre-Talmudic era in Judaism, parables and proverbs served as instructional tools to help youth learn history, culture, tradition, and faith.

Parables offer comparisons of two things for the sake of illustrating a particular point. In the Bible, parables convey a deep, spiritual truth. Irving Jensen declares that parables are "revelation by illustration, giving aid to understanding" (Jensen, 125). It is no wonder then that during His earthly ministry, Jesus told many parables aimed at giving truths to His followers. Jesus used parables as a vehicle of teaching the masses. The parables, therefore, become clear only when one is able to receive the difficult truth they reveal. This is evident where each of the Gospels—as well as the book of Revelation—record some variation of the phrase "He that has ears to hear, let him hear." Parables are the perfect vehicle for helping our spiritual ears to develop so that we can understand and adhere to God's Word.

Searching for Truth examines 10 of the parables of Jesus. The first parable under study is about the house built on a rock. It compares the actions of a wise person with those of a foolish one. This parable appears in both Matthew 7 and Luke 6. While the parable is the centerpiece for this chapter's study, the preceding verses help us understand the parable more fully.

SCRIPTURE TEXT ⁓

> **MATTHEW 7:21, KJV** *Not every one that saith unto me, Lord, Lord, shall enter into the kingdom of heaven; but he that doeth the will of my Father which is in heaven.*
> *22 Many will say to me in that day, Lord, Lord, have we not prophesied in thy name? and in thy name have cast*

out devils? and in thy name done many wonderful works?
23 And then will I profess unto them, I never knew you:
depart from me, ye that work iniquity. 24 Therefore whoso-
ever heareth these sayings of mine, and doeth them, I will
liken him unto a wise man, which built his house upon
a rock: 25 And the rain descended, and the floods came,
and the winds blew, and beat upon that house; and it fell
not: for it was founded upon a rock. 26 And every one that
heareth these sayings of mine, and doeth them not, shall
be likened unto a foolish man, which built his house upon
the sand: 27 And the rain descended, and the floods came,
and the winds blew, and beat upon that house; and it fell:
and great was the fall of it.

BIBLE BACKGROUND ⌒

The end of Matthew 4 explains that Jesus, after calling the
Twelve, began to teach in synagogues throughout Galilee
and to heal people of diseases. His fame spread quickly, so
that by the time of the events in chapter 5, many were finding their way to Him. Chapters five through seven of the
book of Matthew comprise Jesus' "Sermon on the Mount."
The mountain referred to is actually a hillside in Caper-
naum, a region near the Jordan River. Some scholars believe
that this teaching took place over several days. The words of
Jesus recorded in these three chapters are considered to be
"the longest and fullest continued discourse of our Saviour
that we have upon record in all the gospels" (Henry, 2010).
In this sermon, Jesus gives practical and profound advice to
His followers. He also exposes the hypocrisy and false teaching of those in religious power through His preaching on
the "ethics of the kingdom" (Keener, 1993).

Even before the Sermon on the Mount, it was clear to
listeners that the religious leaders had not been conducting
religious, social, economic, or political business in the ways
Jesus was describing. While everyone may have realized a
difference, Jesus left no doubt what He meant. For example,
Jesus clearly rebukes the false teaching of the scribes and
Pharisees and calls followers to a higher standard of obedi-

ence to God (Matthew 5:19–20). In other instances, Jesus repeats phrases such as "It has been said" or "You have heard" and contrasts those by saying, "But I say." These were references to and refutations of the teaching of the leaders of the day. By confronting the religious practices of His time, Jesus preached a powerful prophetic message that was totally different than anyone had heard before. The authority of Jesus' words was clear to everyone who heard His message (see Matthew 7:28–29).

Jesus' message gave His listeners encouragement and hope. The Sermon on the Mount begins by declaring a new status for all who follow the Lord: "Blessed *are…*" Throughout the sermon, Jesus spoke in contrast to what the Pharisees and scribes taught. His message explained and proclaimed what God desires of those who follow Him. Jesus ends His sermon with this parable (Matthew 7:21–27), comparing the foundation upon which a house is built to the foundation upon which a life of following God is built.

EXPLORING THE MEANING ⌒
1. LORD, LORD (MATTHEW 7:21–23)
Jesus begins His final statements of the sermon by declaring that not everyone will enter into the kingdom of heaven. This is a major paradigm shift! For centuries, under the rule of the Pharisees, common folk had found themselves under the thumb of the religious leadership with no hope of being considered acceptable for the Kingdom. In this passage, however, Jesus tells listeners that God has a criterion by which people will enter the kingdom of heaven. The thought that even one Pharisee or scribe might miss the Kingdom was amazing. After all, these were the religious leaders who held the answers to all religious questions. If they weren't all going to make it, who would?

Jesus reinforced His words by explaining that the criterion for entry into the Kingdom was doing God's will. This must have been even more appalling. The implication was clear: God has a will, and only those who comply with His will may enter His kingdom. What then was the will of God?

God's Law obviously reveals God's will. Hadn't the Pharisees and scribes been giving instruction on the Law? Hadn't they written volumes to explain the Law? Surely they understood God's will. But Jesus was saying that there is more to God's will than these leaders perceived and declared. Jesus was giving reference to God's will that the Messiah, the Promised One, God's Son, be obeyed. The Jewish community had long awaited the Messiah who the prophets had declared would come. Now, that Messiah sat on the hillside and taught them God's will.

Jesus' followers understood that in a future time, God would judge all people. John Gill refers to "that day" as "the last day, the day of judgment, the great and famous day, fixed by God, unknown to angels and men, which will be terrible to some, and joyful to others" (*Exposition of the Entire Bible*). Notice that Jesus will be present "on that day," the great day of the Lord's judgment, and that all inquiries and decisions regarding the rewards due to followers will be directed to Him. Jesus Himself will be the Judge. In this message, then, Jesus forthrightly declares who He is and His relationship to God Almighty! Jesus is the One with the power to accept into heaven those who His Father has declared worthy.

Matthew uses the language and imagery of a courtroom to explain this situation. The greeting directed to Jesus at that day will be "Lord, Lord." This is a plea for the leniency. In Greek, the word translated "Lord" is *kurios* (**KOO-ree-os**), which indicates a title of respect. Where those who wish to gain entry on "that day" should be calling on the Lord based on their relationship with Him through obedience to God's will, those described here by Jesus will instead be presenting their case by trying to justify their "good deeds" of prophesying, casting out devils and "many other good works." "Prophesying" (Gk. *propheteuo*, **prof-ate-YOO-o**) refers to people who have stood before the nation and declared themselves to be prophets, able to speak for God and give predictions for the future. "Casting out" (Gk. *ekballo*, **ek-BAL-lo**) "demons" (Gk. *daimonion*, **dahee-MON-ee-on**) is a claim that demonic beings have been ejected by the oath of the claimant.

The final plea will be that all of the "many wonderful works" (i.e. miracles) were performed "in your name," meaning in the name of the Lord. Jesus, however, has already declared that these imposters don't really know who He is although they call Him Lord. Jesus explains that in that day, He will profess that He never—not at any time— knew them! To their horror, Jesus would declare their actions to have been works of "iniquity" (Gk. *anomia,* **an-om-EE-ah**) or sin and demand that they get away from Him!

2. THE WISE MAN (vv. 24–25)

After graphically and forthrightly declaring who will not enter the kingdom of heaven, Jesus speaks in a parable to explain who will enter. In sharp contrast to the lists of actions the Pharisees demanded people keep in accordance to their interpretation of the Law, Jesus provides a parable that addresses the foundation needed to follow in His footsteps. By beginning His parable with the word "therefore," Jesus connects His statements to the previous information about those who will be denied entry into the kingdom of heaven.

In the parable, a wise man is compared to a foolish man. Here, attitude precedes action. The wise man did not become wise because of where and how he built his house. The wise man was wise because he understood where and how to build his house. The word "wise" (Gk. *phronimos,* **fron-IM-oce**) means thoughtful and cautious in making plans and carrying them out. This is more than just being intelligent, smart, or even skillful. This is an inner discipline and way of thinking. Because the man was wise, he considered the reality of what he would face and prepared for it. Jesus explains that the man was prepared for rain, floods, and violent winds. He did not sit and wait, hoping that the rain, wind, and floods would not come. He prepared by building on the rock because he realized that the house would have to withstand these elements.

Jesus then completes the analogy by likening the person

who "hears" (Gk. *akouo*, **ak-OO-o**) and "does" (Gk. *poieo*, **poy-EH-o**)—that is, obeys—the "word" (Gk. *logos*, **LOG-os**) that Jesus speaks. This is more than casual hearing and nodding in assent. This means obedience based on understanding. In this analogy, the words of Christ are the rock. The building is equivalent to obedience, doing what is required to withstand the storms of life.

3. THE FOOLISH MAN (vv. 26–27)

In the second half of the parable's analogy, Jesus says that those who hear His Word but fail to respond appropriately to His Word are foolish. Interestingly, both the wise and the foolish people hear. They both have access to the Word and are given an opportunity to respond. The foolish ones, however, fail to respond. They can be compared to a foolish person who, knowing that the rain will come and the winds will blow, still builds a house on sand.

Sand is far from reliable as a foundation. It is an unsteady and untrustworthy substance. Sand drifts and moves with the pressure of any force against it. Sand is also deceptive. If left alone, it looks solid. It is when the pressure is applied that sand is seen as the unstable force that it is.

Jesus completes the parable by explaining what happens when the circumstances of life come. The house falls! Jesus describes it as a "great" (Gk. *megas*, **MEG-ahs**) fall. The Greek word for "fall" (*pto sis*, **PTO-sis**) indicates a crash. In the Greek, the description is a mega–fall.

CONCLUSION

The word "fall" can also be translated "downfall." This latter meaning seems to speak to what occurs in our lives when we are outside of Christ and are disobedient to God's will. That is when we suffer a downfall. We find ourselves unable to weather the storms. We are unable to remain steadfast or to find our bearings in the struggles of our lives. Our decisions are faulty. Our efforts are unproductive, and we flounder foolishly.

We may find ourselves busy in our churches and in the

"work of the Lord," but today's text reminds us that it is the relationship we have with Christ as His obedient servants who hear and obey His Word that makes the difference in this world and in our lives. Regardless of the hectic schedules we lead and the hurried lives we live, we must dedicate ourselves to building a foundation in Christ and upon the Word of the Lord.

Thank God for Calvary and for Jesus Christ, our Savior, who came that we might have life abundantly (John 10:10). It is not God's will that anyone be lost, and through the sacrifice of Jesus Christ, salvation is free (Matthew 18:14, Romans 6:23). We are blessed that we have the enlightenment of what this parable holds. Those first listeners to Jesus did not have Calvary to help them understand it all.

Today we can acknowledge that this parable begins with salvation and helps us consider how we live our lives in and for Christ. Those who fail to heed and obey the Word of Christ will, in the Judgment, say "Lord, Lord," only to be met with the final gavel of the Judge who will declare that He does not know them. The bottom line is clear: we must be born again, and, having received His Spirit, we are compelled by His Spirit to know Him and to live in obedience to His Word. We are told in this parable to build on a solid foundation of rock. Our Rock is Christ Jesus. It is Jesus Christ, Himself, who is the chief cornerstone.

Let us therefore rejoice knowing that in Christ, the rain may descend, the floods will come, the winds will surely blow and beat upon the earthly tabernacle that we know as our house of flesh. We rejoice, however, knowing that we will not fall because our lives are founded upon the Rock. ,

REFLECTIONS ⌒

1. *Why did Jesus choose a parable about building a house to explain the difference between obedience and disobedience?*
2. *What is the bedrock of your life? Is it family, faith, financial stability, or something else? How does it measure against the parable Jesus shares in this text?*
3. *In what ways and under what circumstances do you ever find yourself saying "Lord, Lord," but resisting total obedience to*

God's will in your life?

DECIDING MY RESPONSIBILITY ⌐

PERSONAL

1. Many people claim difficulty in recognizing God's will for their lives. Whether you believe you understand God's will for your life or not, center your personal devotion time this week on this lesson text and other Scriptures. Spend time reflecting on how your personal desires and actions might best reflect God's will. A few Scriptures to consider are Matthew 7:21 and James 1:22–27.

2. Wisdom is not always an automatic response. Wisdom grows with experience and can be increased by listening to wise counselors. Make a list of the counselors in your life. While the list need not be long, it should include those who can testify to how God has guided them in various situations.

3. If you find your list of wise counselors lacking in spiritual mentors, talk with your pastor or a seasoned believer who will keep your confidence and help you determine how to make sound and wise decisions in a variety of situations. Above all, remember that establishing these types of relationships is based on your personal relationships and may often arise from modeled behavior rather than direct conversation.

4. Consider a decision you've made that was not wise. Prayerfully review your choices to determine:
   a. How might you have demonstrated more wisdom where you acted outside of God's will and Word?
   b. What biblical truths could guide you into more wise actions in the future?

COMMUNITY

1. Work with your Bible study group or friends to organize a multigenerational luncheon that can help establish positive relationships between those who need to identify counselors and those who are considered wise members of the body of Christ.

2. Matthew 8:22 indicates that we can be quite busy in good acts (religious and natural) without really being in God's will. Gather either a prayer partner or a small group of believers with whom you engage in a ministry activity. Engage in a time of prayer and reflection asking God how to insure that your actions are meaningful expressions of His will. Consider:

    a. What might you do before, during, after and between activities to resist a "checklist" approach to ministry responsibilities?

    b. Individually consider your motives for engaging in or joining the ministry. Then seek group support and prayer for any personal decisions to continue or discontinue involvement in this work.

3. Often we engage in ministry activities that are church-centered without giving equal thought to God's requirement that we "go into all the world" to spread the Gospel. Either personally or with others, examine ways you can extend your gifts, talents and resources to join in a community or global effort to assist others who are experiencing spiritual or natural need.

CLOSING PRAYER

Lord, thank You for giving us what we need to stand strong in the midst of our storms. Help us to share the good news of Jesus Christ with others and build solid relationships based on Your Word. Grant us the wisdom to know Your truth and not be deceived by foolishness.

SOURCES

Gill, John. Matthew 7:22 note. *Exposition of the Entire Bible.* E-Sword Electronic Commentary (version 7.6.0). http://www.esword.net (accessed June 28, 2010).

Henry, Matthew. "Commentary on Matthew 5." In e-Sword Electronic Commentary (version 7.6.0). http://www.esword.net (retrieved June 11, 2010).

Jensen, Irving. *Jensen's Survey of the New Testament.* Chicago, IL: Moody Press, 1981. 125.

Keener, Craig. "Matthew." In *The IVP Bible Background Commentary (New Testament).* Downers Grove, IL: InterVarsity Press, 1993. 55.

New Testament Greek Lexicons. Bible Study Tools.com. http://www.biblestudytools.com/lexicons/greek (accessed July 12, 2010).

THE UNFORGIVING SERVANT

Based on Matthew 18:23-35

KEY VERSE ⁓

"FORBEARING ONE ANOTHER, AND FOR-
GIVING ONE ANOTHER, IF ANY MAN
HAVE A QUARREL AGAINST ANY: EVEN AS
CHRIST FORGAVE YOU, SO ALSO DO YE"
(Colossians 3:13, KJV).

OPENING PRAYER ⁓

*Lord, we have grown accustomed to having a bond with
You that is based on grace, but our relations with each
other are based on self-serving principles. Grow us, teach
us, and make us over to know that this dual set of behaviors is unacceptable in Your kingdom. Anoint us with the
spirit of true forgiveness so that we may mirror it and be
living epistles of Your Word. Amen.*

WORDS TO CONSIDER ⁓

1. TALENT (Matthew 18:24). One talent was the equivalent
of between 75 to 88 pounds of silver. It was the largest monetary unit of New Testament times. In biblical days, it would
have taken a common laborer about 15 years to earn wages
equaling one talent. Therefore, it is safe to say that 10,000
talents was a debt of millions of dollars.

2. PENCE (v. 28). This Roman unit of currency is the most
frequently mentioned coin in the New Testament. One
pence was the standard daily wage of the average worker.
The KJV translates it as a "penny" (Matthew 20:2), but it
actually amounted to about 17 cents.

INTRODUCTION ⌒

Two days after a massive oil rig explosion, the Deepwater Horizon sank on April 22, 2010 and began leaking enormous amounts of oil into the Gulf of Mexico. There had never been an environmental disaster of this magnitude in the entire history of the United States; it was actually visible from outer space. Several workers were killed, others were injured, and the loss of wildlife was so great that it may never be correctly calculated.

Immediately following the incident, the blame game began. The U.S. government blamed the company that leased the oil rig—British Petroleum (BP). BP blamed the oil rig's platform owner and operator; Transocean, Ltd. Fingers were pointed at the company that was responsible for the deep water drilling cement services, Halliburton, for the platform collapse after the explosion. The most frequent response from people worldwide was criticism. The number of critics greatly outweighed the number of relief aid workers and volunteers. At one point, the entire tragedy became more political than environmental.

Instead of never-ending blame and criticism, forgiveness is the first step to total recovery. No one loves wildlife more than God does. God's eyes will be upon us in the years of recovery from this crisis. He will be watching how we help in whatever ways we can, how we treat one another, and how we work together with the authorities, always remembering that complete forgiveness is essential. He will be listening to see if we seek heavenly opinions on this and other earthly matters, while continually praying and trusting that when we do all that we are able to do, He will follow up by doing the rest.

SCRIPTURE TEXT ⌒

MATTHEW 18:23, KJV *Therefore is the kingdom of heaven likened unto a certain king, which would take account of his servants.* **24** *And when he had begun to reckon, one was brought unto him, which owed him ten thousand talents.* **25** *But forasmuch as he had not to pay, his lord* *commanded him to be sold, and his wife, and children, and all that he had, and payment to be made.* **26** *The servant therefore fell down, and worshipped him, saying, Lord, have patience with me, and I will pay thee all.* **27** *Then the lord of that servant was moved with compassion, and loosed him, and forgave him the debt.* **28** *But the same servant went out, and found one of his fellowservants, which owed him an hundred pence: and he laid hands on him, and took him by the throat, saying, Pay me that thou owest.* **29** *And his fellowservant fell down at his feet, and besought him, saying, Have patience with me, and I will pay thee all.* **30** *And he would not: but went and cast him into prison, till he should pay the debt.* **31** *So when his fellowservants saw what was done, they were very sorry, and came and told unto their lord all that was done.* **32** *Then his lord, after that he had called him, said unto him, O thou wicked servant, I forgave thee all that debt, because thou desiredst me:* **33** *Shouldest not thou also have had compassion on thy fellowservant, even as I had pity on thee?* **34** *And his lord was wroth, and delivered him to the tormentors, till he should pay all that was due unto him.* **35** *So likewise shall my heavenly Father do also unto you, if ye from your hearts forgive not every one his brother their trespasses.*

BIBLE BACKGROUND ⌒

During the biblical era, King Herod's yearly revenue from taxes for Syria, Samaria, Judea, and Phoenicia was about 900 talents combined. Therefore, one person being in debt for 10,000 talents to another person indicated that this person owed more than he would ever be able to repay. In those days, the inability to pay was justification for confiscation of anything the borrower owned, plus imprisonment and possibly the selling of his family into slavery. Total pardons and forgiveness in these particular situations were unheard of.

Jesus told the parable of the unforgiving servant to explain how important forgiveness is in Christian living. Forgiveness was one of the most important of Jesus' teachings for Christians. The lessons were instructions on how to live until the day of His return.

During this time, the rabbis taught that people should excuse one another's offenses a maximum of three times. But when Peter asked Jesus if seven was enough times to forgive someone who has wronged you, Jesus told Peter to forgive them seventy times seven (Matthew 18:21-22). He was figuratively stating that we should forgive those who sin against us as many times as we would want God to forgive us for sinning against Him.

EXPLORING THE MEANING ⌒

1. WHY JESUS TAUGHT USING PARABLES

Jesus often taught using parables. He used earthly stories that were easy for His audience to relate to so He could get His heavenly point across. This parable was prompted by Peter, who asked Jesus how many times he had to forgive his brother. It's safe to assume that Peter thought he was being both kind and liberal by suggesting seven times. Jesus' response to him must have taken both Peter and the other listeners by surprise. Jesus used the parable of the unforgiving servant to help the listeners understand God's viewpoint.

2. GOD'S LOVE-BASED DEALINGS WITH US (MATTHEW 18:23–27)

Jesus starts this story with a king who was auditing his payment collection books and bringing everything up to date. This was a relatively common occurrence and certainly one that the listeners could relate to. One of the king's servants owed him 10,000 talents, which was more than could be repaid in one's lifetime. He had no recourse, because there was none higher in authority than the king. When he was called upon to pay his debt, he humbly fell down before the king and begged for mercy. He asked the king to be patient and promised to pay it all, although everyone knew it was impossible to repay that amount of debt.

What happened next in the story amazed the onlookers, as it seemed too good to be true. The king didn't give the servant more time, but being moved with compassion, he excused the entire debt. At that time, living under Roman rule, the people knew all too well that the king could do whatever he wanted—but complete amnesty? Wow, Jesus really had their full attention!

3. OUR RULE-BASED DEALINGS WITH EACH OTHER (vv. 28–31)

The listeners also understood that you had the right to go and retrieve what was owed to you. This same servant was owed 100 pence by a fellow servant of his, which was comparable to about 100 days of labor. It would have taken this fellow servant about three months to work off the debt, but it was a debt that could be paid. The fellow servant asked for more time, and realistically a little more time was all that was needed for this debt to be repaid in full.

The servant who had been previously forgiven by the king was merciless. It was almost as if he had immediately forgotten the magnitude of debt that he had just been released from. He did not forgive the debt of his fellow servant, and would not even grant the man a payment extension. The contrast was so appalling that it grieved those who witnessed the whole situation. Jesus was trying to convey how it looks when any one of His disciples refuses to forgive another, especially after God has so graciously forgiven us. God, as the Scriptures say, has abundantly pardoned (Isaiah 55:7).

4. HARVESTING GRACE (vv. 32–35)

Because all of the witnesses reported the behavior of the unforgiving servant to the king, it was obvious that they felt his punishment was much deserved. After all, how could he not forgive an offense so small, when he had been forgiven for so much more? Jesus was drawing His audience in to see the concept of forgiveness from the king's perspective. Jesus previously taught the people quite plainly, "If you forgive those who sin against you, your heavenly Father will forgive you. But if you refuse to forgive others, your Father will not forgive your sins." (Matthew 6:14–15, NLT). This parable brought His divine point home with clarity. Peter, along with all the other disciples, now understood just how important forgiveness is to God and the consequences to believers who refuse to be forgiving.

REFLECTIONS ⌐

1. *Try to remember some instances in your life when you've felt that you were treated unjustly, or have been wronged or hurt by a family member or close friend. Ask yourself, after all was said and done, in what ways have you acted like the unforgiving servant when dealing with people in the past?*
2. *When you are in a position to bestow grace on someone who has mistreated you, how can remembering God's forgiveness help you?*
3. *Why do you think Jesus specified that you must forgive from your heart?*

DECIDING MY RESPONSIBILITY ⌐

PERSONAL

As you look at the devastating and far-reaching effects that the BP oil spill has had on our environment and the world, purpose in your heart to forgive those who have been deemed responsible for the disaster. Recognize that not just the Gulf Coast but the entire country needs the help of every single person to save the environment from total destruction. Be determined to do your part, starting with refraining from carelessness. Remember that your efforts are not short-term fixes; they are the beginnings of lifelong adjustments and enhancements. Here are a few examples of ways to begin this lifestyle change:

1. Don't carelessly pour contaminants in drains and sewers (pesticides, germicides, prescription drugs, bleach, etc.). Read and follow all labeled instructions for proper disposal, or go online to government-sponsored web sites such as http://www.fda.gov and obtain appropriate instructions.
2. Make sure to keep your car's routine maintenance work up to date with things like emissions checks so that you are not frivolously pumping toxins into the air.

3. Carpool as much as possible. Walk or ride bicycles whenever possible.
4. Properly dispose of aerosol cans, batteries, cell phones, and fluorescent bulbs.
5. Winterize your home to aid with energy conservation.

Resources listing these types of proactive approaches are readily available. Contact your local Cooperative Extension for directions and advice on doing your part in these matters.

COMMUNITY

1. As the mistakes and lack of effective emergency procedure preparation of the BP oil spill continue to manifest themselves, as a church community you can use the catastrophe as an opportunity to clean up your local neighborhood while evangelizing to save souls.
   a. As a church body, depending on the size of your church, you may form a clean-up committee to go out and clean your community. Discuss your areas of outreach. Consider possibly covering an area of up to a three mile radius.
   b. Host a community effort that will include sweeping up trash on the streets, raking leaves (seasonally), and clearing gutters. You can even include beautification in these undertakings by planting indigenous trees and community gardens in areas that have fallen into disarray due to apathy.
2. Members can go out in droves, armed with tracts that talk about the saving power of Jesus Christ and our responsibilities to God's green earth. The theme will be forgiveness: helping people see that instead of holding grudges against and not extending grace to the people responsible for environmental disasters, we must first confess and forgive our own environmental negligence. Then we must work together with due diligence to heal an ill environment.

CLOSING PRAYER ⌐

Dear God, Your care for the world is amazing and wonderful. Help us to be better caretakers of the world and one another. In the Name of Jesus we pray. Amen.

SOURCES

Brand, Chad, et al. *Holman Illustrated Bible Dictionary.* Nashville, TN: Holman Bible Publishers, 2003.

Barton, Bruce B., et al. *Life Application Study Bible NIV.* Grand Rapids, MI: Tyndale House Publishers and Zondervan, 2005.

Burdette, Dallas. "Grace Beyond Comprehension," Freedom in Christ, 2001. http://www.freedominchrist.net/Sermons/Parables/Grace%20Beyond%20Comprehension--Matt%2018.htm (accessed June 19, 2010).

"Gospel of Matthew 6 (*New Living Translation*)." Blue Letter Bible. 1996–2010. http://www.blueletterbible.org/Bible.cfm?b=Mat&c=6&t=NLT (accessed June 14, 2010).

3

THE TALENTS

Based on Matthew 25:14-30

KEY VERSE ⁓

"SO THEN EVERY ONE OF US SHALL
GIVE ACCOUNT OF HIMSELF TO GOD"

(Romans 14:12, KJV).

OPENING PRAYER ⁓

*Lord, thank You for the varied gifts and resources that
You have bestowed upon and implanted in each one of
us. Smite laziness and selfishness from our beings so
that we may be determined and work diligently without
distraction, like the burden-bearers in Nehemiah 4:17.
Cause us to grow in wisdom and guide our every step so
that we may fully and correctly use what You have given
us to grow and magnify Your Kingdom. Amen.*

WORDS TO CONSIDER ⁓

1. EXCHANGERS (MATTHEW 25:27). Bankers, creditors,
brokers, money changers; those known for trading currency
for nominal fees. In Israel during the biblical era, the job
of the exchangers became essential because there was a law
requiring every male Israelite over the age of 19 to pay a
half-shekel into the sanctuary's treasure at every census as an
offering to Yahweh. The Jewish people of this time period
came from all over the world. Therefore, the matter of trading foreign coins for all sorts of business and other reasons
became a very lucrative occupation. Jesus ousted them from
the Temple courtyards because of their godlessness and
money-grubbing behavior.

2. USURY (v. 27). The fee charged for a loan; could also be defined as interest. Per Old Testament laws, Jewish people were allowed to charge Gentiles a "usury" (Deuteronomy 23:19-20), but they were not allowed to charge one another. Unreasonable usury charges were heavily frowned upon.

INTRODUCTION ⌒

Two elderly women lived in very nice rental condominiums for persons aged 55 and older. One day they each donated $5.00 to a local Girl Scout troop that annually went door to door asking for donations for their yearly food drive for the poor. About a week later, the ladies were pleasantly surprised to hear that they were the winners of a one-year supply of food from a local supermarket. Unbeknownst to them, everyone who donated to the scout troop on that day had their names entered into a drawing, and from thousands of donors they were awarded this special gift.

Both seniors lived alone. Other than sporadic visits from family members and people from their monthly senior ministry outreach meetings, neither had many visitors. Therefore, this amount of food was entirely too great for either of them to properly utilize all by themselves. Although they did not cook much anymore, both seniors were excellent and very skilled cooks.

The women were happy about receiving such wonderful gifts. They could just barely fit all of the groceries into their kitchens. Their refrigerators, freezers, and pantries were overstuffed to the point of bulging. Once everything had been snugly put away, both women sat wondering what to do with this bountiful blessing.

Finally, one of the ladies decided to just store all of the food as safely as she could, and use it on holidays and any family events that might arise. Ultimately, as time passed, all of the food went bad. She didn't have any room in her condo's kitchen area for the canned goods. She had put them in an outdoor storage shed which flooded after a pipe burst, and even the canned food was destroyed. The food that she packed in the freezer eventually became unrecognizable from freezer burn and also became a total waste. Her freezer broke down from being overstuffed, and after several warnings from the property manager, she was evicted for the foul stench that engulfed the premises from the spoiled food. The other woman prayed and put deep thought into what to do with her gift. She decided to be creative in giving it back to the community from which it came. She made many phone calls, rallying dozens of other seniors to help her plan menus, cook, and distribute food. They turned it into the largest evangelistic event that their area had ever seen. Dozens of cakes were baked, and powerful Scriptures were written on the cake faces with the most colorful and tasty icings. They used church vans and delivered carloads of hot meals to shelters—plastic forks and knives were wrapped in tracts. Her team organized barbeques in neighborhood parks. Trees were draped in large banners which read "FREE FOOD FOR ALL." All the while praise teams sang, praise dancers danced, and speakers gave ongoing messages of salvation.

A local printing company heard of the woman's efforts and donated 5,000 copies of tracts in exchange for 100 homemade pies, which they in turn donated to rape crisis centers and children's hospitals. The gift of the food was used as a mighty evangelisic instrument, and like salvation, it became a gift that kept on giving.

Squander, laziness, and selfishness with divine talents are blatant sins that grieve the Holy Spirit and leads to spiritual death. As ambassadors of Christ, we must not only respect the power and authority that was given to us in His name, but we must also embrace and utilize every gift that He has blessed and entrusted us with.

SCRIPTURE TEXT ⌒

MATTHEW 25:14, KJV *For the kingdom of heaven is as a man travelling into a far country, who called his own servants, and delivered unto them his goods.* 15 *And unto one he gave five talents, to another two, and to another one; to every man according to his ability; and straightway took to his journey.* 16 *Then he that had received the five talents* *went and traded with the same, and made them other five talents.* **17** *And likewise he that had received two, he also gained other two.* **18** *But he that had received one went and digged in the earth, and hid his lord's money.* **19** *After a long time the lord of those servants cometh, and reckoneth with them.* **20** *And so he that had received five talents came and brought other five talents, saying, Lord, thou deliveredst unto me five talents: behold, I have gained beside them five talents more.* **21** *His lord said unto him, Well done, thou good and faithful servant: thou hast been faithful over a few things, I will make thee ruler over many things: enter thou into the joy of thy lord.* **22** *He also that had received two talents came and said, Lord, thou deliveredst unto me two talents: behold, I have gained two other talents beside them.* **23** *His lord said unto him, Well done, good and faithful servant; thou hast been faithful over a few things, I will make thee ruler over many things: enter thou into the joy of thy lord.* **24** *Then he which had received the one talent came and said, Lord, I knew thee that thou art an hard man, reaping where thou hast not sown, and gathering where thou has not strawed:* **25** *And I was afraid, and went and hid thy talent in the earth: lo, there thou hast that is thine.* **26** *His lord answered and said unto him, Thou wicked and slothful servant, thou knewest that I reap where I sowed not, and gather where I have not strawed:* **27** *Thou oughtest therefore to have put my money to the exchangers, and then at my coming I should have received mine own with usury.* **28** *Take therefore the talent from him, and give it unto him which hath ten talents.* **29** *For unto every one that hath shall be given, and he shall have abundance: but from him that hath not shall be taken away even that which he hath.* **30** *And cast ye the unprofitable servant into outer darkness: there shall be weeping and gnashing of teeth.*

BIBLE BACKGROUND ⌒

Spiritual talents and gifts are abilities, strengths, and empowerments that are set apart from one's basic capabilities, because these skills are anointed by the Holy Spirit. Some have more talents than others, but every single Christian has been blessed with spiritual gifts (Ephesians 4:7). There are many different kinds of spiritual gifts. Humans may consider some gifts to be greater than others, but in the eyes of God there is no hierarchy of greatness. The church is one body, and the gifts are to be used for its edification and successful functioning (1 Corinthians 12:14–26).

Divine gifts come from the Holy Spirit. God assigns them for His own sovereign reasons. He endows His people with these gifts as equipment, enabling them to effectively minister to the church body because our congregations have a huge variety of essential needs. Therefore, there clearly would be no benefit to everyone having identical gifts. In His infinite wisdom, God gives us the gifts that we are easily capable of managing (Matthew 25:14–15).

God hates the squander of the gifts that He entrusts to us. When we let things like jealousy, selfishness, and laziness cause us to misuse or bury the graces that He has implanted within us, it displeases Him greatly. The only benefit that comes from this type of wastefulness is to the wickedness of human nature. This kind of behavior grieves God in His heart (Genesis 6:6).

EXPLORING THE MEANING ⌒

1. JESUS USES A PARABLE TO TEACH

This is the second of the three parables that Jesus taught after His disciples asked Him what would be the signal of His return. Jesus taught about the last days in Matthew 24. He followed this up with parables to help them clearly understand how to prepare for His return. He used three different parables, each one teaching what the believer must do while waiting in preparation for His return.

2. TALENTS ARE GIVEN ACCORDING TO PERSONAL ABILITY (MATTHEW 25:14–15)

Jesus' audience could easily relate to a servant who has been left in charge of his master's assets and expected to work to earn an increase for his master in his temporary absence. This was an ideal illustration, because Jesus wanted His listeners to understand that they are servants who have been entrusted with divine goods. God has given everyone varied and valuable "talents"—expertise, time, abilities, artistries, skills and money. Jesus also clarifies that we are not all given the same amount of anything. Some have more spiritual gifts than others, more natural talent, more money, and even more time on this earth. Believers shouldn't compare themselves with others, because God has given us each talents according to our specific abilities. He implanted these endowments within us before we were formed in our mother's womb. He knew us before He placed us there and sanctified us before we came forth (Jeremiah 1:5).

3. DILIGENT SERVANTS ARE REWARDED (vv. 16–23)

Jesus emphasized to His audience that it doesn't matter how much you have. What matters is what you do with what you are given. He knew the natural human propensity to compare quantities (John 2:24). Even believers fall into the trap of thinking that if you have more "talents," you are more important and more loved by God. Jesus makes it clear that that is absolutely not ever the case. Matthew 25:21 and 23 are identical. Both servants gave their master a return on his investment; although the amounts of their increases were different, they received the exact same praise. One servant's return was five talents, while the other's was only two. Yet both had doubled what they were initially given, so their reward was equal. Jesus, in His teachings, has also made it plain that to whom much is given much is required (Luke 12:48).

Each servant stood before his master individually. So, too, will every human being stand naked and defenseless before the eyes of the one to whom we must render an account (Hebrews 4:13). Believers will have to stand before Christ the Son (2 Corinthians 5:10), and non-believers will have to stand before God the Father (Revelation 20:11–15). Every single one of us will be held accountable for our earthly actions, motives, works, and every secret thing. whether good or bad (Ecclesiastes 12:13–14).

4. THE LAZY SERVANT IS REBUKED (vv. 24–27)

People have always made excuses. We see, even in this parable, that the servant who did not do what he was supposed to do made excuses almost confrontationally. He even went so far as to call his master "hard" (v. 24). It seems to be innate in human nature to find a way to blame or project our shortcomings on others. In this case, it was a supposed fear of the master that was the reason why this servant did not make the most of his lord-given "talent."

If we consider this for a moment, perhaps we can see ourselves and understand the error in this servant's thinking. It is possible that he made the common mistake of comparing himself to others. Maybe he went to church with the other two servants and overheard the amount of talents that the master gave them. Maybe he felt that what he received was insignificant because it was less than what the others received. He may have reasoned that he would never be able to accomplish anything noteworthy because everyone was given more than he had been given, so why bother to try? Maybe he never fully understood that God never asks you to be anyone other than yourself—completely missing the fact that his master only expected a return on what was given to him.

If that last servant had doubled the return of his single talent, he would have received the same accolades and rewards as the other two did. He didn't believe what he had was valuable enough to be a vital contribution, so he simply buried it and refused to apply himself to the task before him. He squandered his talent, ultimately cheating himself out of the blessing of reaching his divine potential.

The servant's excuse for not cultivating and multiplying his talent actually wound up condemning him. He confessed that he knew his master's expectation. He couldn't even pretend not to know. The servant knew that the talent was not really his, but was on loan with the expectation that he would use what was entrusted to him. The master called this servant wicked and lazy, which was the actual truth behind why he buried his talent. The master never acknowledged that the servant had called him "hard."

We see this kind of scenario every day. Consider the employees who know what their employment entails, but only do the bare minimum of what they were hired to do. Then when these employees are fired, how many times are they heard complaining about how hard and unreasonable their boss was? The master here was not hard at all. He simply had an agenda and an expectation, which each servant was aware of. His master reiterated that since the servant knew that expectation, he should have done what was called for.

5. THE WORKINGS OF THE ECONOMY OF GOD (vv. 28–30)

There is much to be learned in what happens in these verses. The master takes the one talent from the servant who buried it and gives it to the one who already had 10. Jesus then explains this decision. He teaches that those who are most faithful and diligently use all that God has given them will be given more and will have abundance. Those who gripe and complain about how little they have and how little God has given them will lose even what they already have.

Jesus is teaching believers, who want more that they should faithfully and consistently use, what they already have. If you show yourself trustworthy with the talents that you have been already given, then you will be given more and you will have abundance.

In this parable, Jesus is teaching about the economy of God, which is not a new concept or lesson. Jesus taught this same principle after teaching the parable of the four soils. He taught His listeners to pay close attention to His instruction. The more closely they listened, the more understanding they would be granted; in contrast, those who did not listen, even the little understanding that they had would be taken from them (Mark 4:24–25).

REFLECTIONS —

1. *Have you, in any areas of your life, made excuses about not fully using all of the gifts and talents that God has given to you?*
2. *In what areas do you know that you need to be more diligent and faithful in the use of your spiritual gifts?*
3. *If Jesus were to return today, when you stood before Him, do you believe that He would say, "Well done, good and faithful servant"? If not, what can you purpose to do, starting today, to change this?*

DECIDING MY RESPONSIBILITY —

PERSONAL

As you consider all that God is saying to you in this parable, pray and ask God to show you how you can more actively use the gifts He has given you. Pray and ask God to help you think of ways that you can use your "talents" to help our environment. Be careful not to fall into the trap of comparison. Make a list of your gifts and talents in one column. In the second column, write out how you can use that particular gift or talent to build up and clean up your environment. Some examples may be:

1. I'm a giver—buy flower beds for my neighbors and promote composting.
2. I'm a helper—go out and clean trash off my block or in a local park.
3. I'm bold and outgoing—go door to door to solicit neighbors to help you form a neighborhood clean-up committee.
4. I'm a teacher—interactively teach young and old people in your neighborhood about gardening, cleaning, and methods of disaster prevention. Teach the techniques and benefits of harvesting rainwater.
5. Do the homework and make a detailed list of specialized local recycling centers. Place flyers listing this information in the mailboxes of everyone in your neighborhood.

COMMUNITY

In an effort to use the gifts and talents in the body of Christ, suggest a block beautification project. You may choose the block that your church is on, or one nearby where beautification is greatly needed. Have someone in the group/church make poster-sized sign-up sheets that read, "We need you! What's your talent?" The posters may creatively ask those to sign up with certain gifts. For example:

- Green thumbs needed! Sign up here!
- Helping hands … if you have them, please sign up here.
- Calling all givers! If you understand that it truly is more blessed to give than to receive, sign up here and write your monetary donation.

These are just a few examples that allow people to use their God-given gifts and talents. This beautification project will not only help the community; it also will allow people to work in their area of giftedness, which always has the greatest return.

CLOSING PRAYER

Lord, we know that the final redemption of the body won't happen until Christ returns to claim us, but while we wait help us to recognize and utilize to the best of our ability all of the precious gifts that You have instilled in us for the expansion of Your Kingdom, the exultation of Your Being, and the satisfaction of Your Spirit. Amen.

SOURCES

Brand, Chad, Charles Draper, Archie England, Steve Bond, E. Ray Clendenen, and Trent C. Butler. *Holman Illustrated Bible Dictionary.* Nashville: Holman Bible Publishers, 2003.

"Money-Changers." *International Standard Bible Encyclopedia.* Bible History Online. 1995. http://www.bible-history.com/isbe/M/MONEY-CHANGERS/(accessed June 28, 2010).

4
THE SOWER
Based on Mark 4:2-20

KEY VERSE —

"WALK WORTHY OF THE LORD...BEING FRUITFUL IN EVERY GOOD WORK"

(Colossians 1:10, KJV).

OPENING PRAYER —

Dear God, we welcome Your presence in our search for knowledge and understanding. Allow Your Word to reign in us as we humbly offer ourselves to You as willing vessels fit for this journey. May Your Word be a lamp unto our feet and a light unto our path. Guide us by Your Word along that way that leads to our enlightenment and eternal life. Realize within and through us a fulfillment of Your will and Your heart's deepest desire. Amen.

WORDS TO CONSIDER —

1. PARABLE (Mark 2, 10, 11, 13). "Parable" comes from the Greek *"paraballo"* (**par-ab-AL-lo**), which means, "I place beside" in order to compare. A parable is a form of speech or illustration using a story or saying to teach a lesson. Jesus uses this literary type to reveal knowledge only to those who have the eyes to see and ears to hear.

2. MYSTERY (v. 11). That which is not understood because it has not yet been revealed.

3. FRUIT (vv. 7, 8, 19–20). The expected harvest on seed sown in soil. God expects fruit to come from the Word of God planted in our hearts.

INTRODUCTION ⌒

A middle-aged man was distraught over his wife's stubborn refusal to admit she had a hearing problem. One day he asked his family doctor for advice on how to convince his wife of her hearing problem. The doctor promptly told him that when he got home he could confirm the hearing problem by opening the front door and from there asking his wife what's for dinner.

Then the doctor said, "If she doesn't answer, move closer to the kitchen. Repeat the question," the doctor added, "and if she still doesn't answer, move right up to her ear and whisper, 'What's for dinner, honey?'" In this way, the doctor assured him, she'll have to admit she has the problem.

So the man raced home with joy in his heart and opened the front door. "What's for dinner, honey?" he asked. His wife made no reply, so he moved closer to the kitchen and asked again. "What's for dinner, honey?" Again, nothing. When he looked into the kitchen, sure enough, there she was at the kitchen counter. So, he tiptoed over to her and whispered in her ear, "What's for dinner, honey?" She turned and looked at him straight in the eye: "For the third time, I said, we're having MEAT LOAF!"

Is our hearing as good as we think it is? Good communication requires good hearing. We live in a world whose airwaves are full of signals and sounds seeking to be received and understood. It is not always an easy task holding and discerning the good from the bad.

SCRIPTURE TEXT

MARK 4:2, KJV *And he taught them many things by parables, and said unto them in his doctrine, 3 Hearken; Behold, there went out a sower to sow: 4 And it came to pass, as he sowed, some fell by the way side, and the fowls of the air came and devoured it up. 5 And some fell on stony ground, where it had not much earth; and immediately it sprang up, because it had no depth of earth: 6 But when the sun was up, it was scorched; and because it had no root, it withered away. 7 And some fell among*

*thorns, and the thorns grew up, and choked it, and it
yielded no fruit. 8 And other fell on good ground, and did
yield fruit that sprang up and increased; and brought forth,
some thirty, and some sixty, and some an hundred. 9 And
he said unto them, He that hath ears to hear, let him hear.
10 And when he was alone, they that were about him
with the twelve asked of him the parable. 11 And he said
unto them, Unto you it is given to know the mystery of
the kingdom of God: but unto them that are without, all
these things are done in parables: 12 That seeing they may
see, and not perceive; and hearing they may hear, and not
understand; lest at any time they should be converted,
and their sins should be forgiven them. 13 And he said
unto them, Know ye not this parable? and how then will
ye know all parables? 14 The sower soweth the word.
15 And these are they by the way side, where the word is
sown; but when they have heard, Satan cometh immediately, and taketh away the word that was sown in their
hearts. 16 And these are they likewise which are sown
on stony ground; who, when they have heard the word,
immediately receive it with gladness; 17 And have no root
in themselves, and so endure but for a time: afterward,
when affliction or persecution ariseth for the word's sake,
immediately they are offended. 18 And these are they
which are sown among thorns; such as hear the word,
19 And the cares of this world, and the deceitfulness of
riches, and the lusts of other things entering in, choke the
word, and it becometh unfruitful. 20 And these are they
which are sown on good ground; such as hear the word,
and receive it, and bring forth fruit, some thirtyfold, some
sixty, and some an hundred.*

BIBLE BACKGROUND ⌒

The Gospel of Mark, which is the shortest of the four ca-
nonical Gospels, is also considered to be the oldest and a
primary source for Matthew and Luke. Although John Mark
is identified by many as the author, the Gospel itself does
not specifically identify anyone as its author. The most com-

monly accepted date of its writing is between 66 CE and 75 CE during a period of warfare between Rome and the Jews. A prevailing theme within Mark is called "The Messianic Secret." Jesus is recorded as having on several occasions during His preaching and teaching ministry cautioned His hearers not to reveal His true identity.

Jesus' ministry had suffered a series of public rejections. Thus, Jesus employed the use of parables, a literary type to convey His message while in a mixed audience. Kingdom truths were concealed to those who were "outsiders" but revealed to those who were His disciples. The "parable of the sower" is recorded by all three of the synoptic writers (Matthew, Mark, and Luke), perhaps indicating their concurrence that it played an important part in the teachings of Jesus.

EXPLORING THE MEANING —

1. INTRODUCTION (MARK 4:2)

Both religious and political leaders have been listening to Jesus, but with motives that have been less than sincere. Some are feeling threatened by His growing popularity among the multitudes of people from all walks of life. They have sought to entrap Him, and spies have even been commissioned to follow Him. The religious leaders seek to find something in His teachings that is contrary to traditional belief and acceptance that would bring Him under condemnation and ultimately silencing. The political leaders are motivated by fear of possible insurrection by such a popular but relatively unknown person. Jesus' own family is somewhat embarrassed by His activity. Nonetheless, His popularity continues growing. Crowds are now flocking to hear Him and a small group of persons have become His disciples and left everything to follow Him.

Jesus created quite a stir with His preaching and teaching, and He knows that there is growing opposition to His ministry. Yet truth must be proclaimed, and it must be made clear to those who seek it. Thus in Mark's Gospel, on several occasions, Jesus asks that His true identity be kept secret so that His work might continue without continuous interruptions from His detractors (Mark 1:43–45; 5:43; 7:36; 8:27–30).

Jesus also chooses a literary type called "parable" to both cloak and convey His message. A parable uses earthly things with which people were familiar in order to proclaim divine truths (Romans 1:20). The unknown gets revealed through the known. Through God's creation, through nature and the experiences of life, the mind and heart of God are revealed to the ones who have eyes to see and ears to hear. Jesus quotes Isaiah 6:9–10 when seeking to explain the reason He is using parables to hide divine truths from those who are not true seekers.

2. THE SOWER, THE SEED AND THE SOIL (vv. 3–9)

Mark gives us very few examples of the parables of Jesus in his Gospel, focusing most of his attention on miracle stories and Jesus' encounters with Jewish religious leaders. So when Mark retells one of Jesus' parables, we can have some certainty that in his mind it is significant to our understanding of Jesus' ministry.

Most Jewish people lived in cities and towns. It was not unusual for a farmer to go several miles to the land where he was growing his crops. Farming was different then compared to the straight, orderly rows of crops that today's farmer plants. At that time, a farmer would simply walk through the land set for growing and throw out seed in sufficient quantity to best ensure a good crop at harvest time.

The parable does not speak to the farmer's ability or the seeds' quality. The assumption is that both are good without reason to be challenged. The growth of the sower's scattered seeds depends solely on the quality of the land's condition where it falls. Jesus' parable of the sower illustrates four possible types of land conditions and the fruit that comes from each.

The first soil described is that of the wayside or path. Palestinian farms were unfenced fields through which roads and paths were often made by travelers passing through. The constant traffic would beat down and harden the soil so that any seed that fell upon it would not be able to take root. It would either be crushed underfoot or carried off by birds. The second soil type is rocky ground. Rocky ground has a thin covering of soil, but not enough for seed to become deeply rooted. Perhaps it is on rocky soil, near the beaten down path or land used to collect the rocks removed from other areas, that some of the scattered seed falls. The seed is not able to penetrate deeply into the ground. Without deep roots under the blazing sun, it is unable to draw moisture from beneath the surface. Thus it shrivels up and dies before it has any real chance of surviving.

The third soil type is thorny ground. The Middle East is noted for its many varieties of thorny plants that flourish in the area (see Ezekiel 19:12–13). Some of them are so tall and thick that not even a horse can penetrate them. Seed falling on this ground will soon find itself struggling for life with the hardy prickly plants already existing there. The struggle usually ends with barren results.

The fourth soil type is good ground. It is not hardened, pressed down, or filled with rocks or thorny plants but with fertile soil advantageous to the abundant production of much fruit. A very good harvest would be thirty-fold, an exceedingly good harvest would be sixty-fold, but a hundred-fold would be extraordinarily good.

3. THE MYSTERY OF THE KINGDOM (vv. 10–13)

As Jesus was explaining how His words could elicit so many different reactions from those who had been hearing them, His words even then affirmed the truth of the parable. His own disciples as well as those who traveled in their company did not fully hear and comprehend what He was saying. Like Jesus' mother Mary did, when the angel Gabriel spoke to her concerning her supernatural pregnancy, they "pondered these things" until they could be alone with Jesus. When alone, they want to know why He speaks such holy and divine truth in language that is not plain for everyone to understand.

Jesus' explanation to them appears at first to contradict

the idea that God's truth is for all. "It is to you" He says, that knowledge of "the mystery of the kingdom of God" is given. Rather than Jesus establishing by decree hard lines of division between some who are given what others are not, He is simply revealing what is already in place. Jesus describes the reality that is already in existence. All were given the same word, but all did not hear it in the same way. The parable gives each equal access, but depending on the hearer, the access does not yield the same understanding. Some will hear the words being articulated and see the picture being painted, which is just the outer manifestation of the parable; but not everyone will discern its inner meaning. Thus, some will miss its eternal life-giving truth. Those who truly seek life will be given access to the inner meaning of the parable. Those who only look for trouble, or are deceivers or insincere, will be kept locked outside, only to have contact with the outward casing or apparent literal meaning of the parable in which there is no eternal life.

"Know ye not this parable? and how then will ye know all parables?" How do we know this parable? How will we know any parable? By becoming a truth seeker or disciple. Although Mark does not include it in his Gospel, both Matthew (7:7–8) and Luke (11:9–10) include in theirs these words, "Ask, and it shall be given you; seek, and ye shall find; knock, and it shall be opened unto you: For every one that asketh receiveth; and he that seeketh findeth; and to him that knocketh it shall be opened."

Because His disciples and those that followed along to this gathering place are now alone with Jesus, He gives them understanding of His parable.

4. THE MEANING OF THE PARABLE (vv. 14–20)

In His parable, Jesus leaves no doubt as to the identity of both the sower and the seed. Jesus is the sower, and the seed is His Word, the *Logos* (**log-OS**) that issued from the mouth of Jesus. In Matthew's account, the Word is called "the word of the kingdom" (Matthew 13:19) and in Luke's account it is called "the word of God" (Luke 8:11). Neither the sower nor the seed can be challenged on the basis of ability or quality. The sower and the seed are one and the same in this parable. Jesus and His Word are equal, constant, and without differentiation when sown into the soil. The soil is the human heart. Therein lies the differences that ultimately lead to the type of harvest that shall come. The human heart runs the gamut of good and evil. It must constantly be cultivated, cleared, and cleansed to maintain good receptivity to the Word that would enter in.

The seed or the Word has within it the fruit that can ultimately come forth. What will come forth depends on the heart in which it is planted. The seed of the Word is powerful and intended to be fruitful, for it is full of good things. Jesus explains how the human heart determines what manner of harvest is attained. He answers this for four types of human hearts.

What happens when the Word is sown into a hardened heart? Hearts can be affected deeply by many years of forced servitude, pain, disappointment, despair, or by many years of meaningless existence following an endless routine of rituals, or by a daily diet of perverseness and indifference. The heart becomes so crushed under the weight of such experiences that even when something good, that could be life giving, enters someone's life, the response can be indifferent and quickly denied before the Word can take root. Jesus said that this is what Satan does when the Word is heard by a hardened heart.

What happens when the Word is sown into a rocky heart? These are shallow-hearted persons who only have a thin layer of acceptance for the Word. They are enthusiastic about what they are hearing, very excited by it, but not greatly impacted by it. As soon as some trial, tribulation, or trouble comes, in the heat of the moment they forget what they have heard and wither away. Rather than being made strong by those experiences, they are weakened because they have no deeply rooted memory of what they have heard. They have no connections to a supply of nourishment to steady their growth. This heart is only good for hearing the latest or the next fad or thought that comes along, and it too will only remain briefly.

What happens when the Word is sown into a heart full of thorns? This is a heart with proper, grounding but the grounding is inhabited with unclean, inappropriate, destructive thoughts, ideas, and concepts. In these instances the Word enters and, though it takes root, it is simply one of many incoming words. Over a span of time, the other words choke, stifle, and eventually kill the growth and development of that good Word.

What happens when the Word is sown into a good heart? Jesus gives us the all-important reason for attaining and maintaining what the psalmist asks for: "A clean heart...and...a right spirit" (Psalm 51:10). Jesus says that there is no limit to what it can produce. Normal rules and expectations of what can be achieved are cast away. A new standard is established. The Word growing and developing with our hearts enables us to become entirely new persons who also become sowers ourselves. When the Word is heard, takes root in us, and is allowed to grow and develop, it will become the Word that we shall proclaim for others to hear. Thus the Word multiplies itself in others. What happens in a good heart can be replicated 30, 60, or 100 times as the hearer of the Word is transformed into a sower of the Word, like Jesus.

This parable shows us not only how to gain access to inner meanings of other parables, but also a look at the potential that has been placed in the seed of God's Word that has been given to us.

From Jesus' use of this parable, we discover that Satan, the evil one of the world, uses a double-barreled approach in response to those who have received the Word. It might be called a carrot-and-stick approach. If the Word cannot be easily taken away, then out comes the stick, hardship and tribulation. If the stick doesn't work, the Devil brings forth the carrot—the allure and entanglement of life's riches and pleasures. Satan doesn't miss a trick when it comes to damming up or confusing our hearing. If he cannot shake us by tribulation, he will woo us by the treasures and riches of the world.

REFLECTIONS ⌒

1. *Judgments and decisions are too often made with too little information and insight about an individual or situation. Have you ever done this? Has someone ever done this to you? How did you feel when either of these occurred?*
2. *In light of the four types of hearts expressed in this lesson, can you think of a time when your heart or hearing reflected each of them? What did you do, if anything, to change the state of your heart?*
3. *How do you understand therespond to the thought that the words of Jesus seemingly indicateing that some people are destined to be deaf to the Word (Logos) and thus remain unconverted?*

DECIDING MY RESPONSIBIITY ⌒

PERSONAL

1. Have you been a victim of misunderstanding? Consider times when you said something, that was not heard the way that you meant for it to be heard. You know this because the reaction was far from what a true hearing of your words should have produced. Speaking clearly and hearing with understanding are critically important to good communication. Sometimes you must say the same thing in different ways in order for the hearer to grasp the real meaning of your words.

   When communicating, you choose words that are intended to convey concepts, ideas, thoughts, and feelings; others must then hear those words and interpret their meaning. Hopefully, they come up with the concepts, ideas, thoughts, and feelings that you meant the listeners to grasp.

   Not only do you do that with others around you, it also happens in your communications with God. When God speaks, do you always hear God's Word clearly and perfectly? Who could be a better communicator than God? What can help you hear more clearly?

2. Take some time and reflect back over your life. Determine what for you are the three most significant persons and the three most significant events in your life. They could be good or bad.

Base your choices are on your present understanding that God was using them at that time in your life to speak a word to you. You realized only afterward that you were not hearing God's Word; you know it was God's Word now, but you did not know it then. What were the obstacles that impeded your hearing at that time? Write them down.

3. After doing this, examine your life now, including the people and events that are part of it, and ascertain if the language God used back then is the same language He uses to communicate with you now. What might be keeping you from hearing God clearly and perfectly now? Write down some of the obstacles that you think are blocking your hearing. What are you going to do about the stumbling blocks?

COMMUNITY

God speaks also to communities. These communities may be large or small. Select one of your communities (your close friends, family, church, club, neighborhood, etc.) and determine how God has spoken to them in the past and how they might improve their ability to hear God speaking to them now.

CLOSING PRAYER ⌒

Dear God, we have so much for which we are thankful. You have given us Yourself wholly and completely that we might be made fit for Your kingdom. And You have revealed unto us a way to enter therein and attain the fullness of eternal life. May You grant us Your favor that our walk toward and our work within Your kingdom will bear an abundance of fruit that is pleasing unto You. Amen.

SOURCES

Buttrick, George Arthur. "Mystery, Parable." *The Interpreter's Dictionary of the Bible,* Vol. K–Q. Nashville, TN: Abingdon Press, 1982. 479–480, 649-653.

Henry, Matthew. "An Exposition, with Practical Observations, of the Gospel According to St. Mark." *Matthew Henry's Commentary on the Whole Bible.* Biblos. http://www.biblecommenter.com/mark/4 (accessed July 3, 2010).

Jones, Edgar. *The Parable of The Sower, The Interpretation.* Voice of Jesus.org. October, 2006. http://www.voiceofjesus.org/thesower.html (accessed July 4, 2010).

Loughman, Peter. "Parable of the Sower: God's Word." Sermon Central.com. http://www.sermoncentral.com/sermons/parable-of-the-sower-gods-word-peter-loughman-sermon-on-parable-sower-and-seed-109888.asp (accessed June 29, 2010).

THE GOOD SAMARITAN
Based on Luke 10:30-37

KEY VERSE ⁓
"LET US NOT LOVE IN WORD, NEITHER IN TONGUE; BUT IN DEED AND IN TRUTH"
(1 John 3:18, KJV).

OPENING PRAYER ⁓
Lord, thank You for loving us and showing compassion to us. God, help us to do the same and be loving and compassionate toward all of our neighbors. We lift up this prayer in the mighty name of Jesus. Amen.

WORDS TO CONSIDER ⁓
1. PRIEST (Luke 10:31). An adult male from Aaron's family lineage whose duties involved offering sacrifices to God on behalf of the people of Israel and overseeing the worship in the temple (Smith's Bible Dictionary).
2. LEVITE (v. 32). An adult male descendant from the tribe of Levi who assisted the priest in the worship in the temple (Smith's Bible Dictionary).
3. SAMARITAN (v. 33). A person who lived in the region of Samaria; they were hated by the Jews (Smith's Bible Dictionary).

INTRODUCTION ⁓
During May 2010, 52 counties in Tennessee and Kentucky experienced heavy rains and severe flooding. The media called it the "Nashville Flood," although many other areas were affected by the devastation. Eighteen inches of rain fell

in a span of 36 hours. Many people were surprised by the intensity of the rain. One of the two water treatment plants in Nashville became inoperable, resulting in a lack of clean drinking water.

The widespread flooding distressed all classes of people: young and old, rich and poor, healthy and ill. Although the national media did not pay a lot of attention to the overwhelming situation in the "Volunteer State" and the surrounding areas, the local and regional media took notice with news about the flooding in print, radio and television media.

More importantly, volunteers went to work. Neighbors were helping neighbors and strangers were helping strangers. Volunteers rescued people who were trapped in their homes or their businesses. The volunteers did not just sit back and say, "What a terrible situation." They were not apathetic about the disaster and its effects on the residents. They took action because of what they saw and read, and they decided to become a part of the solution. "National representatives of the Red Cross said when they came to town they didn't have the immediate demands on their resources that they expected because so many people had volunteered their time and supplies to help the victims of the storm that turned neighbors into flood victims" (Sellers, *Huffington Post*, 2010).

When we consider this and other tragedies, whether they result from "natural" disasters or from human-made failures, we should feel compassion for victims of these circumstances. God calls us to put our compassion into action and express our concern to individuals who have needs. Our concern should be physically expressed. God does not want us to just say, "I'll pray for them." Prayer is important. However, God requires us to go out of our way to help others. Furthermore, God does not want us to be parochial in our assistance. We must be willing to help others who do not look like us. We live in a global environment. Events that occur in different countries and on other continents can have wide-ranging and far-reaching effects on our local landscape. At times, we must sacrifice convenience, time and resources to bless someone who is in need. In the process, we are demonstrating love and mercy toward our neighbors.

SCRIPTURE TEXT ⌐

LUKE 10:30, KJV *And Jesus answering said, A certain man went down from Jerusalem to Jericho, and fell among thieves, which stripped him of his raiment, and wounded him, and departed, leaving him half dead.* **31** *And by chance there came down a certain priest that way: and when he saw him, he passed by on the other side.* **32** *And likewise a Levite, when he was at the place, came and looked on him, and passed by on the other side.* **33** *But a certain Samaritan, as he journeyed, came where he was: and when he saw him, he had compassion on him,* **34** *And went to him, and bound up his wounds, pouring in oil and wine, and set him on his own beast, and brought him to an inn, and took care of him.* **35** *And on the morrow when he departed, he took out two pence, and gave them to the host, and said unto him, Take care of him; and whatsoever thou spendest more, when I come again, I will repay thee.* **36** *Which now of these three, thinkest thou, was neighbor unto him that fell among the thieves?* **37** *And he said, He that showed mercy on him. Then said Jesus unto him, Go, and do thou likewise.*

BIBLE BACKGROUND ⌐

In this parable, Jesus was speaking to an expert in the Law concerning the process for attaining eternal life. The parable of the good Samaritan spoken by Jesus is included only in the Gospel according to Luke. The telling of this parable occurred in the Gospel during Jesus' journey to Jerusalem. A lawyer (that is, a scholar of the Law of Moses), who was concerned about inheriting eternal life, approached Jesus because Jesus had been preaching and teaching in various areas during His ministry.

During this conversation, Jesus asked the lawyer what the Law states about achieving eternal life. Because he was an expert in the Law, he should have known the correct response. The lawyer replied that love of the Lord and love of neighbor are both written in the Law. Jesus agreed and encouraged the lawyer to express love to the Lord and love to his neighbor.

In an effort to make sure he followed the Law exactly, the lawyer wanted to know who his neighbor was. He wanted Jesus to tell him precisely. The lawyer probably requested an itemized list so that he would not be compelled to show love to those who were not on the list. He was waiting for a list so that he could tell Jesus, "I have showed love to my neighbor. I have obeyed the Law." So the lawyer asked Jesus a direct question: "Who is my neighbor?"

A direct question deserves a direct answer. The lawyer did not get the answer he was seeking, however. Instead of answering the question straightforwardly, Jesus shared this parable with the man. In fact, Jesus does not answer the question at all.

Instead, Jesus spoke of the inaction of a priest and a Levite when each one encountered an injured man on the road. A Samaritan, however, not only felt compassion but also acted on what he felt. He nursed the injured man during a time when he had an extreme need. At the conclusion of the parable, Jesus asked the lawyer, "Who was the neighbor?"

The purpose of this parable is to teach us that we must demonstrate love and compassion to all people, not just individuals who look like we look or live where we live. Jesus was teaching His hearers about the danger of being narrow-minded and discriminatory. During the days of Jesus' earthly ministry, the Jews hated the Samaritans severely because of their ethnicity. Many of the Jews considered themselves a more pure race than the Samaritans were. The word "Jew" was an ethnic term to describe a person whose ancestors originated in the land of Judah (Leith, 1998). Many of the people who lived in the region of Samaria, however, were descendants of Jews who had returned from the Babylonian exile and married Gentiles. Thus, when Jesus portrayed a Samaritan in a positive light in this parable, He forced the lawyer to view Samaritans as people, not as objects worthy of hate, discrimination, or scorn.

EXPLORING THE MEANING ⌒

1. THE ROAD TO JERICHO (LUKE 10:30)
Jericho, also referred to as the "city of palm trees" in the Old Testament (Deuteronomy 34:3; 2 Chronicles 28:15), was a city located east of Jerusalem and west of the Jordan River. Jesus does not tell the lawyer anything about the man who was on the journey to Jericho; He does not mention the man's age, ethnicity or socio-economic status. The lawyer may have assumed that Jesus was speaking about a Jew. In fact, many commentators maintain that the injured man in the story was, in fact, a Jew. Jesus, however, merely described the traveler as "a certain man." The 17-mile road from Jerusalem to Jericho was a steep and winding descent. That road was probably quite difficult to travel because of the great angle.

Because of the numerous caves that were present along the road to Jericho, thieves, murderers, and others with ill intent could hide and wait for unsuspecting travelers to cross their path. The thieves who stripped, robbed, and wounded the traveler may have been hiding in one of those caves waiting for the opportunity to attack someone.

2. UNSYMPATHETIC PRIEST AND UNCONCERNED LEVITE (vv. 31–32)
Jesus did not say why the priest or the Levite were traveling to Jericho. When the priest saw the injured man, he went out of his way to cross the dangerous, steep, winding road to avoid contact with him. When the Levite encountered the wounded man, he actually "looked on him" (v. 32). However, he did the same as the priest and crossed the road to avoid connecting with him. The priest may have thought that the wounded man was dead; he would have become ritually unclean if he had touched a dead body. If this had been the case, nothing would have prevented the priest from alerting someone else about the injured man's plight.

As part of the religious elite of ancient Israel, the priest and the Levite should have known that the Law commanded them to love their neighbor. The wounded man had a concrete need when the priest and the Levite encountered him. Unfortunately for the injured traveler, the priest and the Levite both disobeyed that basic commandment. The priest did not try to help in any way, shape, or fashion. Likewise, the Levite kept on traveling to his destination. The inaction of these holy men showed that they were unsympathetic and unconcerned about the wounded traveler's situation.

3. KINDHEARTED SAMARITAN (vv. 33–34)

There is a lot to learn from Jesus' use of a Samaritan as the vessel through whom the wounded man was blessed. Samaritans did not follow the Jewish Law. Although Samaritans adopted the Pentateuch (the five books of Moses) as their Law, they did not adhere strictly to the provisions. Because of severe Jewish bias against Samaritans, the lawyer would have expected the Samaritan to ignore the injured man. In fact, the lawyer probably did not expect for the next person in Jesus' story to be a Samaritan. He probably expected Jesus to mention that another Jew encountered the wounded man on the road.

This was not the case, however. Not only did the Samaritan feel compassion for the wounded traveler, he acted on his feelings. His mercy and compassion moved the Samaritan to take care of the man's cuts, scratches, and scrapes. The Samaritan willingly used his own resources of wine, oil, and fabrics to clean, treat, and dress the wounds. The alcohol in the wine cleaned the man's wounds. The oil soothed the pain and expedited healing.

Additionally, the Samaritan added extra weight to the back of his donkey by placing the injured traveler on top of the animal. The Samaritan was able to navigate all of those activities while securing his personal safety from any potential criminals. Furthermore, the landscape of the road itself made the Samaritan's activities even more precarious. Despite the inconvenience caused by the presence of the

injured man and his needs, the Samaritan put his agenda
to the side and took care of the wounded traveler.

4. TRUSTWORTHY SAMARITAN (v. 35)

Verse 35 provides the reader with even more insight into
the background of the Samaritan, as well as into the relationship between the Samaritan and the innkeeper. The
Samaritan sacrifices his personal resources by giving the
innkeeper "two pence" so the innkeeper could take care
of the injured traveler. At that time, two pence was approxi-
mately equivalent to two days' wages.

The Samaritan must have known that the innkeeper
would provide appropriate care to the wounded man.
Moreover, the fact that the innkeeper agreed to care for the
hurt man shows that the Samaritan was likely to keep his
word. The Samaritan said that he intended to return to the
inn and that he would reimburse the innkeeper for whatever
he spent above the two pence. The innkeeper believed both
of those statements. The Samaritan may well have had
regular contact with the innkeeper through which he had
proven his trustworthiness.

5. A GENUINE NEIGHBOR (vv. 36–37)

Jesus turned the question back onto the lawyer by asking
him which person in the story behaved like a neighbor.
The answer is clear: the Samaritan demonstrated neighborly
love to the injured man. However, because of the extreme
animosity and contempt that Jews held for Samaritans, the
lawyer could not bring himself to say, "The Samaritan was
the neighbor." Instead, he referred to the Samaritan indi-
rectly by describing him as "He that showed mercy" (v. 37).
Jesus ended the discussion by admonishing the lawyer to go
and demonstrate love and mercy like the Samaritan did with
the wounded traveler.

REFLECTIONS ⌐

1. *How have you been in a position of need similar to that of the
man on the road to Jericho and someone blessed you with*

assistance?

2. *How have you felt when encountering the needs of others who were different from you in race, ethnicity, socio-economic status, etc.? How willing were you to meet those needs?*

3. *How can God transform our hearts so that we will demonstrate compassion and mercy to our neighbors?*

DECIDING MY RESPONSIBILITY ⌒

PERSONAL

Many people feel that they should just mind their own business. Some think that it is too much trouble to reach out and help others who are in need. Even if we do not have much money, all of us have the ability to give our time and our talents. Sometimes, we do not want to get involved with helping people because we think that if situation were reversed, we would not get help from others. Unfortunately, this line of thinking perpetuates the cycle of indifference. Why not start a clothing or food pantry by partnering with an organization?

Consequently, our society as a whole experiences enduring harm. For instance, when a violent crime is committed, witnesses are reluctant to cooperate with the police for fear of being labeled a "snitch." Inherent in this label is a threat of bodily harm to the witness or the family of the witness. This disheartening situation has extended to nonviolent crimes and other offenses that are illegal or immoral. Christians who witness these events are left in a quandary. One way to combat this cycle of indifference is for us to say something when we see something. Many cities and states offer a toll-free telephone hotline as an avenue for sharing information anonymously with law enforcement officials.

Additionally, participating in mission trips in the United States and around the world is another way to break the cycle of indifference. Christians can offer assistance to people with severe needs. For example, the 7.0-magnitude earthquake in Haiti in January 2010 left tens of thousands of Haitians without adequate food, clothing, hospitals, medicine, schools, water, shelter, and sanitation. Before the earthquake, Haiti was the poorest country in the western hemisphere. Months after the damage occurred, the Haitian people were still struggling to re-establish some semblance of normalcy in their homeland. In addition to donating money to the Red Cross, many people have obtained training so they can travel to that country to help rebuild that nation. The country will not be rebuilt quickly. Thus, opportunities still exist to help our brothers and sisters in Haiti. Select an organization where you can help others who have been devastated by natural disasters.

COMMUNITY

Many occasions exist on the community level to demonstrate compassion and mercy to our neighbors.

1. On the neighborhood level, for instance, you can create a "Neighborhood Watch" group where residents can meet and discuss the events on their street.
2. Investigate whether your employer would allow you to volunteer during your work hours without having to use your personal, illness, or vacation time.
3. Organize a group of your colleagues to volunteer collectively. You can arrange a group of first responders who would be immediately available to help people in a community-wide disaster.

CLOSING PRAYER —

God, please give us the courage to speak against situations of injustice. Grant us the ability to act during circumstances of prejudice and discrimination. Lord, transform our hearts so that we can please You as we express love, compassion, and mercy toward others who are in need. We pray this in the Name of Jesus. Amen.

SOURCES

Leith, Mary Joan Winn. "Israel Among the Nations: The Persian Period." In *The Oxford History of the Biblical World*. Edited by Michael D. Coogan. New York: Oxford University Press, 1998. 276–316.

Sellers, Bob. "What the Media Missed in the 'Nashville' Flood." *Huffington Post,* May 10, 2010. http://www.huffingtonpost.com/bob-sellers/what-the-media-missed-in_b_570686.html (accessed June 28, 2010).

Smith, William. "Levite." *Smith's Bible Dictionary.* McLean, VA: MacDonald Publishing Co., 1948. 357–359.

— —. "Priest." *Smith's Bible Dictionary.* McLean, VA: MacDonald Publishing Co., 1948. 532–533.

— —. "Samaritan." *Smith's Bible Dictionary.* McLean, VA: MacDonald Publishing Co., 1948. 583–585.

6

THE RICH FOOL

Based on Luke 12:16–21

KEY VERSE ⁓
"LAY UP FOR YOURSELVES
TREASURES IN HEAVEN"

(Matthew 6:20, KJV).

OPENING PRAYER ⁓
*Dear Lord, thank You for this wonderful opportunity to
study Your Word. Help us to grow and draw closer to You.
Amen.*

WORDS TO CONSIDER ⁓
1. FOOL (Luke 12:20). This word describes an individual
who lacks wisdom; wisdom is beyond his or her grasp (Vine,
1999).
2. RICH (v. 21). Having an abundance of possessions and
material wealth (Merriam-Webster, 2010).

INTRODUCTION ⁓
Money has always been a hot-button issue in the Bible and
in the world. Our country lives and dies by the "almighty"
dollar. It is ironic that "In God We Trust" appears on our
currency, when in fact we often place our trust in the currency itself. People place so much emphasis on money that
some hoard it while others envy those who have it. Afflu-
ence is a disease, spawned by greed, which has corrupted the
hearts and minds of so many throughout history.

In today's lesson, you will learn about a rich man who
was blinded by his prosperity and lost sight of God. Wealth

isn't necessarily a bad thing, but when it hinders our relationship with the Lord, it can be eternally destructive. "For the love of money is the root of all evil: which while some coveted after, they have erred from the faith, and pierced themselves through with many sorrows" (1 Timothy 6:10, KJV).

SCRIPTURE TEXT ⌒

LUKE 12:16, KJV *And he spake a parable unto them, saying, The ground of a certain rich man brought forth plentifully:* **17** *And he thought within himself, saying, What shall I do, because I have no room where to bestow my fruits?* **18** *And he said, This will I do: I will pull down my barns, and build greater; and there will I bestow all my fruits and my goods.* **19** *And I will say to my soul, Soul, thou hast much goods laid up for many years; take thine ease, eat, drink, and be merry.* **20** *But God said unto him, Thou fool, this night thy soul shall be required of thee: then whose shall those things be, which thou hast provided?* **21** *So is he that layeth up treasure for himself, and is not rich toward God.*

BIBLE BACKGROUND ⌒

As Jesus was speaking in front of a large crowd, a man asked Jesus to settle a dispute. The man was upset that his brother would not split his inheritance with him. He felt entitled to half of his brother's inheritance and wanted Jesus to command his brother to fork it over. It is not clear why the man wanted half of the inheritance. Perhaps he was poor, or perhaps he was in debt. Either way, the man was greedy and felt entitled to it for some reason. During this time, the firstborn son typically received his father's inheritance. It is unclear whether the man was the firstborn or not—presumably not—but the main issue was his greed.

Upon hearing the man's request, Jesus refused and warned him against greed. He said that the meaning of someone's life does not consist of material possessions. Jesus then illustrated His point by telling the story about the rich fool.

EXPLORING THE MEANING ⌒

1. A BUMPER CROP (LUKE 12:16–17)

Jesus began to tell the story of a rich man who experienced a bumper crop. Since the rich man did not expect an abundance of crops, he was not prepared to store it all. His barns were too small. Typically, people would find this to be a good problem to have. At least it is a better problem than not having enough crops to survive, but there is some urgency to this issue. If the rich man did not find an ample place to store his crops, the exposure to the elements would cause them to rot or they would be vulnerable to thieves and wild animals. If the rich man had focused on storing up heavenly treasures, he would not have needed to worry about these things. "But lay up for yourselves treasures in heaven, where neither moth nor rust doth corrupt, and where thieves do not break through nor steal" (Matthew 6:20, KJV).

In this story, it is obvious that this rich man is not righteous. "He coveteth greedily all the day long: but the righteous giveth and spareth not" (Proverbs 21:26, KJV). He never considered distributing his crops to other people. He simply intended to keep everything for himself and lead a lazy life. The rich man did not even consider tithing or giving his first fruits to the Lord, who provided him with this great abundance. "Every man shall give as he is able, according to the blessing of the LORD thy God which he hath given thee" (Deuteronomy 16:17, KJV). "Honour the LORD with thy substance, and with the firstfruits of all thine increase" (Proverbs 3:9, KJV).

2. EAT, DRINK, AND BE MERRY (vv. 18–19)

After considering his dilemma, the rich man thinks he has found a solution. He plans to tear down his current barns and construct larger ones. At first, this seems reasonable. When a plant outgrows its pot, you place it in a bigger one. When a business outgrows its facilities, it moves to larger ones. This is a natural response to growth, but the rich man does not mention anyone else in his desire to expand his estate. He's only thinking of himself. "Then said Jesus unto his disciples, Verily I say unto, That a rich man shall hardly enter into the kingdom of heaven. And again I say unto you, It is easier for a camel to go through the eye of a needle, than for a rich man to enter into the kingdom of God" (Matthew 19:23–24, KJV).

Since the rich man has plenty of food and goods stored up, he thinks he will be able to kick back and relax. Perhaps he thinks he's earned an early vacation or retirement. Unfortunately, his trust is not in God but in his wealth. He is not trusting in the fact that God will provide for him. Instead, he is trusting in the bumper crop that he already has, which he does not credit God for giving to him. "But they that will be rich fall into temptation and a snare, and into many foolish and hurtful lusts, which drown men in destruction and perdition" (1 Timothy 6:9, KJV).

3. RICH TOWARD GOD (vv. 20–21)

At this point, God calls the rich man a fool (v. 20). In the previous verses, the rich man revealed his motives, and God was not pleased. Then God reveals to the rich man that his life will end that very night. It is unclear what will cause the man's demise, but this must have been a startling revelation. The Scriptures do not reveal to us whether the man begged for forgiveness, because this would take away from the point of the story.

Not only was the rich man's physical life in jeopardy, but so was his spiritual life. By worldly standards, the man was rich, but by God's standards, he was poor. The world's riches are temporary, but heavenly treasures are eternal. God asks the rich man what will happen to all of his wealth once he is gone. Within His question, God makes an implication about earthly wealth. "For we brought nothing into this world, and it is certain we can carry nothing out" (1 Timothy 6:7, KJV). What is the point of focusing on things that will fade away with time when you could be focusing on God, who is eternal?

Take, for example, the early Egyptians (Mazar, 1992). They buried their pharaohs with all of their possessions because they believed they could take everything with them into the afterlife. Of course, this was not the case, and since that time, thieves and scholars have plundered the tombs. As Jesus said, "Lay not up for yourselves treasures upon earth, where moth and rust doth corrupt, and where thieves break through and steal: But lay up for yourselves treasures in heaven, where neither moth nor rust doth corrupt, and where thieves do not break through nor steal: For where your treasure is, there will your heart be also" (Matthew 6:19–21, KJV).

REFLECTIONS ⌒

1. *How do you define "treasures in heaven"? How does one acquire these treasures?*
2. *What kinds of earthly treasures are distracting you from focusing on God?*
3. *How can you focus more on God rather than on earthly possessions?*

DECIDING MY RESPONSIBILITY ⌒

PERSONAL

1. Take some time to evaluate your life and your goals. Create a list of everything that distracts you from God. Perhaps you need to clean out your life and remove the idols. Money, career, prestige, addiction, sports, unhealthy relationships, and material possessions can all be idols. If any of these things are taking priority over your relationship with God, then you need to reprioritize and possibly remove these things from your life. Create a plan to reprioritize your life and remove the idols that are hindering your relationship with God. Consider having an accountability partner to help you. If your idols involve an addiction of some sort, you may want to seek professional help in order to overcome it.

2. Here is a list of Scripture references that discuss the topic of idols.

Genesis 35:2
Exodus 20:3–5

Exodus 20:23
Leviticus 19:4
Leviticus 26:1
Deuteronomy 27:15
2 Kings 18:4
Psalm 115:4–5
Isaiah 42:17
Romans 1:22–23, 25
1 Corinthians 8:1–13
1 John 5:21

COMMUNITY
Get together with your neighbors or a small group of people from church. Have each family take inventory of their possessions. Suggest they clean out their basements, attics, closets, and garages. Then have the families sort through everything and donate items to various charities, shelters, and thrift stores. You may want to consider having a neighborhood garage sale or a church rummage sale and donating the proceeds to a particular charity or a family in need.

Here is a list of Scripture references that discuss the topic of giving.

Deuteronomy 15:10
Deuteronomy 16:17
Proverbs 3:27
Proverbs 11:24–25
Proverbs 22:9
Proverbs 28:27
Matthew 6:3–4
Mark 12:41–44
Luke 3:11
Luke 6:38
Acts 20:35
James 2:15–16

CLOSING PRAYER ⌒

Dear Lord, thank You for all the blessings You have given us. Help us to focus more on You and Your Son, Jesus Christ, instead of on earthly treasures. We have sinned and fallen short. Help us to remove the idols from our lives in order to see You more. Amen.

SOURCES

"Fool," *Merriam-Webster Online Dictionary.* Merriam-Webster, Inc. http://www.merriam-webster.com/dictionary/fool (accessed June 16, 2010).

Mazar, Amihai. *Archaeology of the Land of the Bible: 10,000–586 B.C.E.* New York, NY: Doubleday, 1992. 277–291.

Vine, W. E., Merrill Unger and William White, Jr. *Vine's Concise Dictionary of the Bible.* Nashville, TN: Thomas Nelson, 1999. 239.

THE PRODIGAL SON

Based on Luke 15:11–32

KEY VERSE ⌐
"FOR YE WERE AS SHEEP GOING ASTRAY;
BUT ARE NOW RETURNED UNTO THE
SHEPHERD AND BISHOP OF YOUR SOULS"

(1 Peter 2:25, KJV).

OPENING PRAYER ⌐
Our Father and Our King, call us through Your Word into
the tenderness of Your heart. Where we are soiled and unclean, meet us, silencing our self-contempt with Your love.
Where we are hypocritical and arrogant, find us, breaking
our self-righteousness with Your compassion. Wherever we
are, whoever we may be, name us Yours. Amen.

WORDS TO CONSIDER ⌐
1. SON (LUKE 15:11, 19, 21, 24-25, 30-31). The blood-re-
lationship that establishes an individual's identity as part of
a larger family and the legal status of bearing and honoring
the father's name (Freidrich, 1972).
2. RECKLESS (v. 13). Careless and wasteful, with a "wild
and disorderly" lifestyle, self-destructive and hopeless; it
implies luxury, but not immorality (Kittel, 1964).
3. SERVED (v. 29). Literally, "slaved." It is "a service that
is not a matter of choice" and "subject…to an alien will"
without rights or freedom; often a derogatory term (Kittel,
1964).

INTRODUCTION ⌒

Henri was exhausted. He'd been working as a professor at
an Ivy League school. The job left him nervous, stressed, and
unsure about his direction in life or even who he was. At
the urging of some friends, he took time to refocus. While
he was visiting a friend, he noticed a poster of Rembrandt's
famous painting, *The Return of the Prodigal Son*. The picture
fascinated him, drew him in, stirred his heart.

He began to study the painting and the story behind it.
These led him, he later recalled, "to an inner place where
I had not been before. It is the place within me where God
has chosen to dwell. It is the place where I am held safe in
the embrace of an all-loving Father who calls me by name
and says, 'You are my beloved son, on you my favor rests'"
(Nouwen, 1994).

Henri left his job at the university. He spent the rest of
his life as a caretaker for the mentally disabled. His encounter with Rembrandt's painting and his meeting with the
story of a father and his sons transformed him.

This chapter will look at that story.

SCRIPTURE TEXT ⌒

> **LUKE 15:11, KJV** *And he said, A certain man had two
> sons:* **12** *And the younger of them said to his father, Fa-
> ther, give me the portion of goods that falleth to me. And
> he divided unto them his living.* **13** *And not many days
> after the younger son gathered all together, and took his
> journey into a far country, and there wasted his substance
> with riotous living.* **14** *And when he had spent all, there
> arose a mighty famine in that land; and he began to be in
> want.* **15** *And he went and joined himself to a citizen of
> that country; and he sent him into his fields to feed swine.
> **16** And he would fain have filled his belly with the husks
> that the swine did eat: and no man gave unto him.*
> **17** *And when he came to himself, he said, How many
> hired servants of my father's have bread enough and to
> spare, and I perish with hunger!* **18** *I will arise and go to
> my father, and will say unto him, Father, I have sinned*

against heaven, and before thee, **19** *And am no more worthy to be called thy son: make me as one of thy hired servants.* **20** *And he arose, and came to his father. But when he was yet a great way off, his father saw him, and had compassion, and ran, and fell on his neck, and kissed him.* **21** *And the son said unto him, Father, I have sinned against heaven, and in thy sight, and am no more worthy to be called thy son.* **22** *But the father said to his servants, Bring forth the best robe, and put it on him; and put a ring on his hand, and shoes on his feet:* **23** *And bring hither the fatted calf, and kill it; and let us eat, and be merry:* **24** *For this my son was dead, and is alive again; he was lost, and is found. And they began to be merry.* **25** *Now his elder son was in the field: and as he came and drew nigh to the house, he heard musick and dancing.* **26** *And he called one of the servants, and asked what these things meant.* **27** *And he said unto him, Thy brother is come; and thy father hath killed the fatted calf, because he hath received him safe and sound.* **28** *And he was angry, and would not go in: therefore came his father out, and intreated him.* **29** *And he answering said to his father, Lo, these many years do I serve thee, neither transgressed I at any time thy commandment: and yet thou never gavest me a kid, that I might make merry with my friends:* **30** *But as soon as this thy son was come, which hath devoured thy living with harlots, thou hast killed for him the fatted calf.* **31** *And he said unto him, Son, thou art ever with me, and all that I have is thine.* **32** *It was meet that we should make merry, and be glad: for this thy brother was dead, and is alive again; and was lost, and is found.*

BIBLE BACKGROUND

Jesus fought marginalization. He taught that God loved everyone and anyone, that His love didn't wait for someone to deserve it. So Jesus ministered to social outcasts—to prostitutes and crime families, homeless people and the disabled. His life exemplified His teaching, showing compassion and solidarity to the marginalized, the irreligious, and the oppressed (Nouwen, 1994).

This infuriated the organized religion of His day. The Pharisees were a sect committed to being as upright and devout as physically possible. They were appalled to hear Jesus actually suggest that God's love wasn't meant to be earned, that God loved people less devout than them. They raged against His teaching of acceptance with the worst complaint they could find: "This man spends time with sinners, and has dinner with them!" (see Luke 15:2).

In response, Jesus told three stories. One of them we know as the parable of the prodigal son. But by the usual conventions of storytelling, it seems Jesus thought of it as "The Tale of the Man with Two Sons." In one sense, the man symbolizes God, with one son symbolizing "proper" people and the other son symbolizing "outcasts." In another sense, it is simply and profoundly a story about a father who showed his sons what love really is, and, by showing them, shows us. Perhaps most truly of all, it's both.

EXPLORING THE MEANING ⌐
1. THE YOUNGER SON (LUKE 15:11-24)

We call him "the Prodigal." We like him, this rebel. We like his courage and his chutzpah, his revolt against the world. We see in him, perhaps, our own youthful arrogance and our own youthful mistakes. It's easy to live the story with him, resting in the comfort of his return.

While he may seem the prototypical young rebel, a closer examination reveals the unsettling contours of a selfish child. He is spiteful and vindictive. He is shrewd and manipulative, yet unable to forecast the results of his actions. He lives without contingencies, clinging desperately to the thread of his own logic.

His story begins like a fairy tale we may have heard. The farmer's second son says to his father, "Give me a sack of silver coins and three red apples—I'm off to seek my fortune!" The younger son sets off through the woods, as it were, his mind awakening to imaginative possibilities. The remoteness of the "far country" parallels the strangeness of the woods, an enchanted kingdom (Luke 15:13). On a quest for self-identification, he pursues a dream-world, hoping to find a merrier dwelling than his father's house.

But the woods are not to be entered rashly or with evil intent. As much as we want to empathize with the younger son's individuality, we can't ignore that he begins his journey under a shadow. "Father, give me the pending allotment of the property" (see Luke 15:12). The younger son's first speech is cuttingly precise. Though he addresses his father with a respectful title, his demand is sharp. These are the imperious words of a master barking at his slaves, not a dutiful son addressing the head of household.

In the culture of this story, the father determines inheritance. An inheritance is never realized until the father has died, and it is never realized at a son's request. By asking to receive the inheritance, the younger son has demanded that his father drop dead (Bailey, 1976). His escape into the far country, removing himself from his father and his family, effectively realizes that demand.

The younger son enters his utopia on the wings of a death wish. Once there, he squandered his household with a freewheeling lifestyle (see 15:12–13). A son was expected to live in a way that honored his father's name (Burke, 2005). This son does not. He lives and spends as though his father had already died.

It is not said here that the younger son is living immorally; until the older son accuses him of soliciting prostitutes, we have no reason to believe he's anything other than extravagant (Bailey, 1976). The story tells us merely that he is over-spending. He extends himself beyond his means and descends into a private hell until "a mighty famine" ravages the far country (15:14). The enchanted paradise of independence becomes the horrors of fiscal liability.

The younger son has revolted against his identity as his father's son and the perceived oppression of belonging to his father's household—the commandments of his father, the hierarchical superiority of his older brother. But he has revolted in the wrong direction. His change in status and location does not liberate him as he hoped, but binds him in a more terrible oppression from which there seems no escape (Freire, 1993).

He then sets in motion his own downward spiral. He descends from being a landed heir within a family household to being a disregarded swineherd, cut off from his entire nation by his uncleanness (Bailey, 1976; Forbes, 1999). He has lost himself; his self-identity and the props he used to establish it are gone. The cunning rebel who demanded "Give, give!" is given nothing. And, the story explains, "No one gave to him" (see Luke 15:16). Thus, he is dehumanized.

The story could end here, with the younger son bereft, a stern warning to honor one's parents. But it doesn't. The sudden turn of the story comes with the younger son's second speech. He "came to himself"—that is, he resumes his identity as a son of a household (15:17). He casts aside his reinterpretation with its insistence on his individual financial liberty, and reviews his situation as though he were still in his father's house.

Carefully assessing his options, he reasons to improve his situation while retaining his independence: as a hired servant, he is a freeman, but retains the benefits of being associated with his father's household (Bailey, 1976). He rehearses his third speech and mentally prepares himself for his reunion with his father. His narrative ends with him limping hopefully and apprehensively back down the long road home, repeating his little speech and clinging to the last shreds of his dignity. At the gates, his father will be waiting—willing, perhaps, to give to him again.

But "you're just settling down with the happy ending when the elder brother appears on the doorstep" (Williams, 2008).

2. THE OLDER SON (vv. 25–32)
He is the firstborn. He is the primary heir. He holds the birthright. But does he go around asking for an early inheritance? Does he abandon his father, his family? Does he do

anything other than keep every household rule and work without complaint?

He doesn't want us to think so. The older son takes some pains throughout the story to distance himself from his younger brother. He insists that he holds a moral high ground while the younger son grovels in debauchery. He will even deny his blood-relation (15:30).

But the differences between them aren't as stark as their circumstances suggest. Remember, the father "divided his assets between them" (15:12). The older brother received a larger cut than his brother did (Forbes, 1999). That is, he benefited from his brother's sin, while neither urging against it nor facilitating repentance (Bailey, 1976). Then he has the gall to rail against the sin once there is reunion made simply through love—without him. He emerges as a hypocritical, shameless devotee of self-benefit and material gain.

The older brother enters the narrative rather late. The dramatic reunion has played out. The party is on. He can hardly be blamed for his lateness, however. The story makes it clear that he "was in the field" (15:25). He's been working, contributing to the upkeep of the household, doing what a good son should do.

The moment he enters, however, he demonstrates his similarity to his younger brother. He too relies on his wits and his reason, shrewdly attempting to assess the situation before he acts. He interrogates a local boy for an account of the day's events, insisting on a full explanation of the hulla-balloo inside (15:26–27). This is not acting like a son who's come home and discovered an unexpected party. This is act-ing like a nosy neighbor looking for a reason to complain to the police. "He is unnaturally suspicious" (Bailey, 1976).

The reason for the party throws him into a fury. "He was angry, and would not go in" (15:28). He offers no explana-tion, sends no apology. He simply lets his absence make his rage conspicuous—thereby deeply insulting his father (Bailey, 1976).

Perhaps, after all, the older son's anger is understand-able. Certainly he didn't part with his brother on the best of terms. His brother has humiliated the family. It may have been a long day in the field—he would be tired, perhaps, wanting a quiet moment to himself. Who wouldn't be annoyed at finding out there's a party they weren't invited to?

These justifications evaporate, however, when the older son speaks his mind. Unlike his prodigal brother, he stays silent most of the story. He speaks only once, venting the frustration and arrogance that have shaped his conduct. His litany of complaints suggests that he has stewed long over these perceived wrongs. In a grotesque inversion of the younger son pondering a reunion with his father, the older has pondered a separation.

His speech is harsh, accusing. He disrespects his father more than his brother ever did, neglecting to even call him "father" (15:29–30). Nor, as we might expect, does he complain that the brother has humiliated the family. After listing his own virtues, he complains that his father has personally humiliated and wronged him. "He has just insulted his father publicly and yet is able to say, 'I have never disobeyed your commandment'" (Bailey, 1976). It seems his father's honor means little or nothing to him. His own honor means everything.

His opening speech reveals the source of this startling diatribe. "Look, all these years I've slaved away for you!" (see 15:29). His self-identity, even as the older son and heir, is "slave" and not "son." He has adopted the same mentality of oppression that spurred his younger brother's revolt. Instead of following his brother's shameful example, however, he has embraced the oppressive system and exploited it to gain power and respect. When he discovers that the system of merit and reward which he has imagined does not, in fact, exist, he reacts with fury.

"Yes," he tells his father in effect, "this oppressive system does exist and I am its slave. You cannot rob me of the rewards I insist I deserve. I will not be reduced to equality with my brother. I will not relinquish my right to make myself who I understand myself to be."

The older son rages with thwarted prejudice. He—and he only—accuses his brother of having "devoured thy living with harlots" (15:30, KJV). He will not see the actual persons of his brother or his father. He sees only a preconceived, vilified idea of what his brother should be within the system of oppression. His own mental oppression approves and affirms that idea (Park, 2009).

His slander reaches its pitch when he calls his brother, "this son of yours" (15:30, NLT). The accusation casts suspicion on his father's morality, and on the younger son's right to the inheritance he's already received. The older son has construed a world where he inhabits a superior caste free from wrong, segregated from his father and his brother through their attempt to establish a new order of relationship.

Despite living in his father's house and scrupulously keeping—even interpreting and applying—his father's commandments, the older son is as far from his father as his brother ever was. He inhabits a mental pigsty of arrogance, prejudice, and hypocrisy that alienates from the love and reconciliation before him. He, like his brother, has adopted an oppressive self-definition that dehumanizes himself and those around him.

If we are honest with ourselves, we understand the older son as deeply as we do the younger. We recognize in him our own arrogance, our own prejudice, our own hypocrisy. We wonder, dismally, whether we too have shunned our brothers and sisters, whether we too might not get the reward we think our merit deserves.

We are, as Rowan Williams points out, "left with that uncomfortable question which Jesus undoubtedly wants his audience to bear in mind, '…what if I'm also the self-righteous nuisance?'" When we stand with the older son, Williams explains, "we have to inhabit the most uncomfortable place of all, the place of the person who doesn't yet know love, or need or patience, and is yet the most needy person, the most deeply suffering person in this story" (Williams, 2008).

But this is not just a story about the older son. This is not even a story about the younger son. This is the story of the man with two sons, and the words he speaks over each of them.

3. THE FATHER

He's rejected. He's insulted and humiliated. He's accused of being an oppressor, told he's better off dead. Yet something draws him to the threshold of his house. Something brings him to the gate to strain for the sight of a familiar figure limping along the road. Something tears him away from his celebration and his guests to reason with an unreasonable rebel.

His actions startle us. There is no restraint in his behavior, none of the decorum which we think would suit his gray hairs and dignified position. Unlike his intellectual sons, he acts with impulse and emotion, deciding radical courses of action without long deliberation. When his younger son assaults him with a death-wish, we expect anger, furious rejection of the shameful demand. Instead he gives.

He gives, in fact, more than was asked. The younger son simply asked for the property to be divided. The father gives him the right of deposition as well. "Not only will I give you your part of the household," the father says, "I will give you full rights of access—it is yours to do with as you see fit." In a wild, unprecedented gesture, the father bestows everything he can upon this rebellious disgrace of a son—more, even, than was demanded (compare Bailey, 1976).

Yet what we would call foolish extravagance facilitates his son's return (Eastman, 2006). Perhaps the most moving image of the story is that of the father running with the recklessness of a much younger man, catching his grubby, pig-reeking, rebellious son in a crushing bear hug. The translation explains simply that the father "had compassion" (15:20). However, the Greek word for "compassion" (*splagcnivzomi*, **splangkh-NID-zom-ahee**) indicates gut-wrenching, stomach-churning emotion. The depths of the father's being pour out in overwhelming love for his son. This welcome heals and restores his son. So the younger son's careful plan dissolves in simple acceptance of love. The well-prepared speech trails away into silence.

For the father, nothing is done well unless it's done hugely. His over-the-top behavior continues. His son must have a robe—the best one—and a ring, and new shoes. There must be a feast—kill the prize calf, invite the village, invite everyone! There must be food for a week and then another week more. There must be music and dancing and everything, three celebrations at once, why not, after all— "This is my son!" (see 15:24).

And then he leaves the party.

He was so excited about everything: all the joy and laughter and food, and all his guests. He even leaves his newly restored younger son. He goes outside. The same ferocity of love and affection that inspired him to throw the party in the first place inspires him to spend it sitting on the porch, trying to reason with an angry, ranting, self-righteous prig. Because—prig or not—this, also, is his son. And as the father knows no boundary in his actions, he knows no boundary in his love.

"His heart," writes Nouwen, "goes out to both of his sons; he loves them both; he hopes to see them together as brothers around the same table; he wants them to experience that, different as they are, they belong to the same household and are children of the same father" (1994).

If this story were a fairy tale, who would the father be? He is not a fairy tale father. They usually vanish once their sons leave to find a fortune. This father reenters with a crash. He is not the frantic, beleaguered king, anxious to marry off his daughter to any deserving adventurer that can vanquish the local giant. He is not the wise old mentor, who helps the hero on his way, but usually isn't with him at the end.

The father's role is more important in this story than all of these. In a sense, through the largeness of his character, he transcends it. He is in the story. But he is also the storyteller. The father only speaks twice. His words conclude both the narrative of the younger son and the older son. The similarities between the two speeches are obvious. The differences are haunting.

He does not speak directly to the younger son, but addresses the servants. It may be that his son already understood him, did not need to hear in words what his father's embrace had already told him (Bailey, 1976). Perhaps the father felt he did not need to tell his son what he tells the servants. He instructs them to treat his son as a son of the household deserves: "This is my son—he never stopped being my son—so treat him like it!" (see 15:23–24).

The father's cry is not simply affirmation, though it is that. It is a claim. He names the younger son his own. He would have the whole world hear his declaration—"This is *my son!*" His words change the younger son's story. Where a moment before, the younger son was unclean, disgraced, and an outcast, he is now, again, the lawful son of a wealthy landowner. The transformation is instantaneous. It is not simply a return. It is a re-creation.

The father does speak to his older son. In face of the older son's flagrant disrespect, the father speaks with gentleness. His words are kind, even tender. "Child, you are always with me, and all that is mine is yours" (from 15:31, ESV). While he shouted to the world the younger son's official, legal identity, he speaks to his older son directly with an affectionate childhood name—"laddie" or "kiddo" might capture the sense of the word here (cf. Forbes 1999). He speaks words of acceptance and healing, an infinitely patient reminder to his older son of who, in fact, he is. "I do not give anything to you," the father says, "because you have it. You're my little boy—you'll always have everything I have to give. Now help me give it away" (see Eastman, 2006).

Significantly, the father says to the older son, "This [is] your brother" (15:32). He reaffirms the blood-relation the older son wants to deny by saying "This son of yours" (NLT), and calls the older son back from self-imposed isolation into a welcoming family. "*We* should celebrate"— that is, the three of us, the father and his two sons (see 15:32, emphasis added). As the younger son has returned, so the father calls his older son to come home. He restores to him his rightful place in the story.

"He was dead, and is alive again; he was lost, and has been found" (15:24, 32). The repeated phrase, like the chorus of a song, brings the story back to its center. The two sons were bound in mental oppression that pitted them against their father and each other. One attempted to overthrow it; the other attempted to exploit it. Neither questioned it. Both assumed the oppression was there. They suffer humiliation and loss of identity because their minds are fixed in a destructive, hopeless narrative. They're in the wrong story.

The father speaks a new narrative to both of them. His words bring "something new into the world" (Williams, 2008). The words are an act of hope, liberating his sons by removing their oppressive system of thought altogether. He invites them to build a new home with him, where "the disappeared will be found, the missing welcomed home, and there will be, finally, no need for distinctions between the 'have-nots' and 'haves'" (Park, 2009). As the storyteller, the father tells a true story, one that transforms its hearers. He proclaims them not slaves but sons, not enemies but brothers, and welcomes them into the new home of his love.

The story ends abruptly. There is no conclusion, no moral, no epilogue, "no happy ending" (Nouwen, 1994). There is simply a "sharp cut in the endless tapestry" of story, a sudden turning of the way; the scene has vanished, the players are gone (Tolkien, 1966). And yet something has happened. "You're not the same at the end as at the beginning" (Williams, 2008). We are left with a resonance of love, an echo of hope, and we are haunted with the memory.

REFLECTIONS ⁓

1. *Which character in this parable do you relate to most? Why? What would it be like to be another character?*
2. *Is there a mentality of oppression in your thinking? What does Jesus' story tell you about it?*

3. *What does the story illustrate about God's love? For you? For others?*

DECIDING MY RESPONSIBILITY ⌒
PERSONAL
Examine your attitude toward God. Has a mentality of oppression influenced your choice of church activities, or your treatment of other people, or your spiritual practices? Reflect on what Jesus says about God's love for you. How will your attitudes and actions change if you really accept that love? Are there people you can show that sort of love to?

COMMUNITY
Are there "prodigals" in your area who need to see God's love for them, the way the sons in this parable needed to see their father's love? Find programs that help social outcasts—homeless shelters or rehabilitation centers, for instance, or caretaking services for the elderly or disabled. Get together with a friend or your study group, and find ways you can help.

CLOSING PRAYER ⌒
Thank You, God, for loving us so much, even in our rebellion. Thank You for saving us through Your Son, Jesus Christ. Amen.

SOURCES

Bailey, Kenneth E. *Poet and Peasant: A Literary Cultural Approach to the Parables in Luke.* Grand Rapids: William B. Eerdmans, 1976.

Burke, Trevor J. *Adopted into God's Family: Exploring a Pauline Metaphor.* Downers Grove, IL: InterVarsity Press, 2005.

Eastman, Susan. "The Foolish Father and the Economics of Grace." *The Expository Times* 117, no. 10 (July 2006): 402–405.

Forbes, Greg. "Repentance and Conflict in the Parable of the Lost Son (Luke 15:11–32)." *Journal of the Evangelical Theological Society* 42, no. 2 (June 1999): 211–229.

Freire, Paulo. *Pedagogy of the Oppressed.* Revised Edition. Translated by Myra Bergman Ramos. London, UK: Penguin, 1993.

Friedrich, Gerhard, ed. *Theological Dictionary of the New Testament.* Translated by Geoffrey W. Bromiley. Vol. VIII. Grand Rapids, MI: Wm. B. Eerdmans, 1972.

Kittel, Gerhard, ed. *Theological Dictionary of the New Testament.* Translated by Geoffrey W. Bromiley. Vols. I-II. Grand Rapids, MI: Wm. B. Eerdmans, 1964.

New Testament Greek Lexicons, Bible Study Tools.com. http://www.biblestudytools.com/lexicons/greek (accessed July 13, 2010).

Nouwen, Henri, J. M. *The Return of the Prodigal Son: A Story of Homecoming.* New York, NY: Doubleday, 1994.

Park, Rohun. "Revisiting the Parable of the Prodigal Son for Decolonization: Luke's Reconfiguration of *Oikos* in 15:11–32." *Biblical Interpretation* 17 (2009): 507–520.

Tolkien, J. R. R. *The Tolkien Reader.* New York, NY: Ballantine, 1966.

Williams, Rowan. "An Address Given by the Archbishop." The Archbishop of Canterbury. June 8, 2008. http://www.archbishopofcanterbury.org/1922 (accessed June 15, 2010).

THE RICH MAN AND LAZARUS

Based on Luke 16:19–31

KEY VERSE ⌒
"CHOOSE LIFE, THAT BOTH THOU AND THY SEED MAY LIVE"
(Deuteronomy 30:19, KJV).

OPENING PRAYER ⌒

Lord, we know that You are ever present with us. In our journey through time and space, we are never alone or without the necessities required to walk our path. Help us to stay conscious that our duty is to walk in Your image and likeness and according to Your will, so that in this world whether ours is a lesser or a greater path, it will always be walked Your way. Keep us forever in Your path, we pray. Amen!

WORDS TO CONSIDER ⌒

1. ABRAHAM'S BOSOM (LUKE 16: 22). It is the place where the good go at the moment of death and where judgment is enacted as preliminary to the final judgment at the end of the age.

2. HELL (v. 23). Greek *Hades* (**HAH-dace**). It is the place of the dead where in New Testament understanding those go who deserve to undergo punishment and torment.

3. REPENT (v. 30). Greek *metanoeó* (**met-an-o-EH-o**). To change one's mind or purpose; implied is the idea that after thoughtful consideration a change is intentionally made from one state of mind or purpose to another.

INTRODUCTION ⌒

During a broadcast of his radio program in April, 1986, Larry Burkett spoke of a young couple who wanted to buy a home, but felt it would be too expensive for them. They told God, "If You want us to buy it, (1) have the contractor accept only half of what he's asking for the down payment, and (2) have the bank approve our loan." Both events happened, and they bought the home. They soon began to go into debt. Their problem: What to do now, since God "directed" them to do this?

SCRIPTURE TEXT ⌒

LUKE 16:19, KJV *There was a certain rich man, which was clothed in purple and fine linen, and fared sumptuously every day:* **20** *And there was a certain beggar named Lazarus, which was laid at his gate, full of sores,* **21** *And desiring to be fed with the crumbs which fell from the rich man's table: moreover the dogs came and licked his sores.* **22** *And it came to pass, that the beggar died, and was carried by the angels into Abraham's bosom: the rich man also died, and was buried;* **23** *And in hell he lift up his eyes, being in torments, and seeth Abraham afar off, and Lazarus in his bosom.* **24** *And he cried and said, Father Abraham, have mercy on me, and send Lazarus, that he may dip the tip of his finger in water, and cool my tongue; for I am tormented in this flame.* **25** *But Abraham said, Son, remember that thou in thy lifetime receivedst thy good things, and likewise Lazarus evil things: but now he is comforted, and thou art tormented.* **26** *And beside all this, between us and you there is a great gulf fixed: so that they which would pass from hence to you cannot; neither can they pass to us, that would come from thence.* **27** *Then he said, I pray thee therefore, father, that thou wouldest send him to my father's house:* **28** *For I have five brethren; that he may testify unto them, lest they also come into this place of torment.* **29** *Abraham saith unto him, They have Moses and the prophets; let them hear them.* **30** *And he said, Nay, father Abraham: but if one went unto them* *from the dead, they will repent.* **31** *And he said unto him, If they hear not Moses and the prophets, neither will they be persuaded, though one rose from the dead.*

BIBLE BACKGROUND ⁓

The authorship of the Gospel of Luke is an often disputed topic among scholars. Some believe it is the work of an anonymous writer, while others believe the writer to be Luke, a close companion of the Apostle Paul. While the writer does not claim to have been an eyewitness, he does claim to have investigated the stories and is reporting his understanding of the life and ministry of Jesus (Luke 1:1-4). He writes with the purpose of explaining the faith more fully to Theophilus, to whom he addresses the account in an orderly manner. Scholars agree that the writer used Mark's Gospel as a source, along with other written and oral sources.

Steadfastly, Jesus has been teaching as He goes through towns and villages on His way to Jerusalem. Although some of the Pharisees tell Him that He should leave town because Herod is planning to kill Him, Jesus continues to teach, drive out demons, and heal people, because that is what He has come to do. In this parable, Jesus addresses the Pharisees who ridicule His teachings about materialism and money (Luke 16:14). They believe their wealth and possessions are a sign of God's favor over others. Jesus condemns their choosing of material possessions over compassion for the poor. This story expresses that while there is nothing wrong with living well and having all of life's finery, one must not neglect the responsibility to do good with what one has been given.

EXPLORING THE MEANING ⁓

1. INSULT ADDED TO INJURY (LUKE 16:19-21)

At a gate known for being part of a wealthy area, Lazarus lay in misery, while dogs licked his sores. These dogs were not pets; in the first century Middle East, dogs were considered unclean. Licking Lazarus' sores did not provide comfort to him but further aggravated his misery.

2. REVERSAL IN POSITIONS (vv. 22–23)

In Jewish culture, a proper burial was important, especially for those of great wealth and status. Both men died; the rich man is buried in the same manner in which he lived. Yet, there is no mention of Lazarus even receiving a proper burial.

In death, the rich man finds himself in hell while off in the distance he sees Abraham, the father of the Jews, with Lazarus lying in a position of honor in his bosom. Their roles in life have now been reversed. The rich man is now suffering and in pain, while Lazarus is now in a place of rest with the beloved Abraham.

3. A CRY FOR MERCY (v. 24)

Upon seeing Abraham, the rich man asks for what he had never shown to Lazarus: mercy. Still believing he is superior, he requests that Lazarus be sent to relieve his suffering. His request is not grand; he only desires a small taste of water to cool his hot and dry tongue. This contrasts with Lazarus lying at the rich man's gate only desiring the crumbs from the lavish table of delicious foods.

4. REMEMBER YOUR CHOICES (vv. 25–26)

The rich man does not receive the response that he hoped for from Abraham. Instead, he receives a reminder of how life was prior to his death. While he lived in comfort, now Lazarus lives in comfort in death. In life, they were separated by the gate of the rich man's home, while in death they would be eternally separated by a great gulf. Only this time, Lazarus would be on the side of the gulf that provided the comfort of good things. Unfortunately, unlike the gate that separated them in life, this great divide between them does not allow for passage between the two.

Abraham's response to the rich man does not indict him for his great wealth in life. However, it implies that he has come to this place of torment in death due to his selfishness in providing only for himself. Although he had plenty, he neglected the obvious needs of Lazarus who lay at his gate.

5. SUFFICIENT WARNINGS (vv. *27–31*)

The rich man makes a second request of Abraham, now showing concern for his brothers who are still alive. He requests that Abraham send Lazarus to warn them about hell so that they may be spared of the rich man's fate in death. However, Abraham replies that the Old Testament teachings of Moses and the prophets were sufficient to serve as their warning.

This answer must have taken the rich man by surprise, yet he continued to plead his case further by suggesting that his brothers would repent and change their lives if Lazarus were to return from the dead. Abraham again responds that if they will not listen to the warnings of Moses and the prophets, who they loved and revered, most certainly they would not listen to someone who returns from the dead. In other words, they had sufficient warning, as did he, that had been provided through Moses and the prophets.

Jesus paints a picture of an unnamed rich man who is adorned with the finery of the day—expensive purple clothing made of luxurious linen material—while Lazarus, full of sores, lay at his gate to beg for crumbs. The actual condition of Lazarus is made clear with Jesus' use of the word "laid" (16:20), which means that he did not simply walk to the gate but was carried and placed there daily. He lay there day after day, at the rich man's gate, desiring to be fed, but was not.

But in all Jesus' parables, only one character is ever given a proper name: Lazarus. Unlike "the rich man" or "a certain man" or even "the prodigal son," Jesus insists on showing Lazarus as an individual person with a real name and dignity. Perhaps He even borrowed the name of one of His good friends (see John 11:5) to suggest that this was a special person whom He cared for. This lesson, and the fate of the rich man who ignored it, show us that it is wrong to dehumanize people from any class or to look on them as insignificant and unimportant. God cares for the rich and the poor alike and knows them all by name. He calls us to love our neighbors the same way.

REFLECTIONS ⌒

1. *We live in a world where there is great disparity of wealth. There are persons and classes of people who have much more than you do and far less than you do. Can you identify a time in your life when you were in the relative position or class of the rich man and of Lazarus? What were your thoughts and feelings toward people in the opposite class?*
2. *Consider all you know about the "afterlife" as portrayed in the parable. What impact does it have on the decisions you now make on how you live your life? Write at least three of those decisions that are influenced by your view of the afterlife.*
3. *True repentance is an act of being truly sorrowful for your actions and consciously deciding to cease from those actions and begin to act a different way. What is the relationship between repentance and consequences? If God gave you the authority to change anything about this story, what changes (if any) would you make? Why?*

DECIDING MY RESPONSIBIITY ⌒

PERSONAL

A multitude and a diversity of blessings from God have been given to all. None of us are without gifts or talents or resources of one kind or another. Caring and sharing can be understood as fundamental to good personal conduct that creates healthy communities.

1. Certainly, God cares and shares to all of humanity. A discerning eye can readily see the evidence for this. How do you see this occurring in your life? Write down some of this evidence of God's caring and sharing from your past and present experiences.
2. Mentors are needed for youth, and advocates are needed for the poor and seniors. Many youth need caring adults willing to share their lives with them. Many seniors are at home by themselves or can't pay for medications. Single parents need financial and emotional support raising their children.
   a. Identify a mentoring organization, social action group, or ministry, and volunteer your support in some way. You may provide administrative, transportation, culinary, counseling, financial, in-kind, or other support of your choosing.
   b. After time has passed, examine your efforts. Do you feel that

these actions have helped you become less like the rich man in the parable and more compassionate to your neighbors? Why or why not?

COMMUNITY

Near our churches are schools that are often looking for assistance with their students. Parental involvement is very important to a child's education but many students do not have adequate support. A caring adult can make a significant impact on students' lives. If your church or an organization you belong to does not have a formal mentoring program operating, initiate the process of starting one. You can begin by talking about this with church or organization leaders and members. Go by yourself or find two or three other caring adults to accompany you, and visit a local school to discuss how such a program could be implemented.

CLOSING PRAYER ⌒

Lord, we thank You for the grace and mercy that You have shared in great abundance over the course of our lives. Thank You for opening our eyes while it is yet time that we might see how to walk in a more excellent way. Thank You for extending Your heart and hand to us and through us. Lord, thank You for giving us another day. We offer this day to You. Amen!

SOURCES

Buttrick, George Arthur. "Abraham's Bosom." *The Interpreter's Dictionary of the Bible, Vol. A-D.* Nashville, TN: Abingdon Press, 1982. 21–22.

——. "Repentance." *The Interpreter's Dictionary of the Bible, Vol. R-Z.* Nashville, TN: Abingdon Press, 1982. 33–34.

Green, Joel B. *New Testament Theology: The Theology of the Gospel of Luke.* New York, NY: Cambridge University Press, 2004. 91.

Henry, Matthew and Thomas Scott. "Luke 16:19." *Matthew Henry's Concise Commentary.* Oak Harbor, WA : Logos Research Systems, 1997.

Jamieson, Robert, A. R. Fausset, and David Bro wn. "Luke 16:21." *A Commentary, Critical and Explanatory, on the Old and New Testaments.* Oak Harbor, WA: Logos Research Systems, Inc., 1997.

9
THE PERSISTENT WIDOW

Based on Luke 18:1–8

KEY VERSE ～
"MEN OUGHT ALWAYS TO PRAY, AND NOT TO FAINT"

(Luke 18:1, KJV).

OPENING PRAYER ～

Dear Lord, teach us to pray. Teach us to hope in You when our lives seem hopeless. Teach us to keep trusting in You when we want to give up. Teach us to love justice and work against injustice. Teach us to believe Your promises and rest in You. Amen.

WORDS TO CONSIDER ～

PERSISTENCE. The character quality of continuing resolutely in a course of action in spite of hardship or opposition.
UNJUST (Luke 18:6). From the Greek *adikos*, **AD-ee-kos**, having an unrighteous heart that is reflected in unfair actions that violate God's Law.

IINTRODUCTION

Everyone faces oppression. Even in America, the "land of the free," the struggles go back for generations. Perhaps our ancestors were slaves, treated as subhuman. Maybe they were immigrants who struggled to earn a living under signs reading, "No Irish need apply." Perhaps they were Native Americans betrayed by deceptive treaties and forced to leave their homes.

You can still talk with people today who vividly remember being relegated to a second-class "Colored Only" restroom, hotel room, or restaurant, denied equal treatment just because of their skin. Or think of apartheid, the struggle for civil rights, racism, sexism, ageism, class distinctions, genocide, human trafficking, and generational poverty. Wherever you come from and wherever your ancestors came from, at some point we've all faced the reality that not only is life unfair, but life is especially unfair to people like us.

In the face of injustice, unfairness, and suffering, can we really believe in a God who answers our prayers?

SCRIPTURE TEXT ⌒

> **LUKE 18:1, KJV** *And he spake a parable unto this end, that men always ought to pray, and not to faint;*
> *2 Saying, There was in a city a judge, which feared not God, neither regarded man: 3 And there was a widow in that city; and she came unto him, saying, Avenge me of mine adversary. 4 And he would not for a while; but afterward he said within himself, Though I fear not God, nor regard man; 5 Yet because this widow troubleth me, I will avenge her, lest by her continual coming she weary me.*
> *6 Then the Lord said, Hear what the unjust judge saith.*
> *7 And shall not God avenge his own elect, who cry day and night unto him, though he bear long with them?*
> *8 I tell you that He will avenge them speedily. Nevertheless when the Son of man cometh, shall he really find faith on the earth?*

BIBLE BACKGROUND ⌒

In Israelite society, widows were seen as vulnerable. They had lost their husbands who would ordinarily have been able to protect them and provide for them. God's Word commands us to show compassion and charity to widows as we would to all those in need. The Law of Moses promises blessings on those who care for widows and punishment on those who do not (Exodus 22:22–24; Deuteronomy 14:29). Paul gave Timothy painstaking guidelines on how his church should support widows in need (1 Timothy 5:3–16).

If a judge, leader, or other authority figure allowed widows to be oppressed, it was seen as a glaring example of injustice (Deuteronomy 27:19; Isaiah 10:1–2; Matthew 23:14). By evoking these concerns in His parable of the unjust judge, Jesus drew on His listeners' sense of the deep injustice that often exists toward the needy and the disenfranchised.

EXPLORING THE MEANING ⌒

It wouldn't be surprising if everyone reading this parable could recall a time they were rejected, hurt, in pain, and facing an unanswered prayer. Even in the Bible, God's beloved "chosen people," the Jews, often seem to be chosen only to suffer as slaves, as exiles, and as wilderness wanderers. Surely they had to wonder, as Tevye the milkman wryly asked God in *Fiddler on the Roof*, "I know, I know. We are Your chosen people. But, once in a while, can't You choose someone else?"

Tevye's question is whimsical, but underneath it lies the real and desperate uncertainty that gnaws at our sense of justice. Why? Why does it have to be this way?

Why, if there's a God who loves us and wants us to be free, do we have to suffer through hatred and restriction? Why does overturning oppression take so long? Why do we have to fight so hard against it if God is on our side? Does God even hear our prayers? Why doesn't He answer them? Is He there?

In the midst of life-and-death questions like these, religious clichés like "Just keep praying!" or "You've got to have faith!" can sound almost insultingly glib. Where is the place for faith and prayer in a world that's seen the Jewish Holocaust, the Cambodian Killing Fields, and the Rwandan genocide? What about your own life, perhaps mild by comparison, but without an end to suffering in view however much you pray? Is there really a purpose to believing in a God who says He wants justice, especially when it seems like He doesn't always get around to acting on it?

1. JESUS BEGINS HIS STORY (LUKE 18:13)

Always a master storyteller, Jesus addressed questions like these by telling tales that turned people's expectations upside down. As a Galilean Jew in first-century Israel under Roman rule, He was no stranger to oppression, discrimination, and hardship. Jesus' story about injustice—known sometimes as "the parable of the unjust judge" or "the persistent widow"—is not at all what we expect, especially if we make the mistake of thinking that the meaning is completely obvious.

It certainly seems obvious. Uncharacteristically, the Gospel writer (Luke) even starts his account by telling us the moral of the story. Parables normally explain their lessons at the end or leave them for us to figure out on our own. To introduce this one, Luke informs us, "Now He was telling them a parable to show that at all times they ought to pray and not to lose heart" (Luke 18:1, NASB).

That sounds suspiciously like a "spoiler" giving away the ending of a movie: "It's a romantic comedy about a girl who decides she should marry her childhood friend instead of a handsome stranger." Has Luke just ruined the ending of Jesus' parable? Not exactly. Sometimes knowing what's coming can take the fun out of a surprise, but other times it can help us navigate the story more clearly or keep us from worrying unduly about the fates of the people involved. In this case, Luke seems to be telling us, "Remember, Jesus really did think that prayer is effective, even though in His story you're about to hear, there's a lot of discouragement and injustice."

As Luke presents it, Jesus' lesson has two contrasting but complementary instructions: We should always be diligent in prayer, and we should never allow ourselves to give up. These instructions are clearly two sides of the same coin: Prayer can keep us from discouragement, or discouragement can keep us from prayer.

However, the points are also distinct. Jesus does not say, "Pray without losing heart." Instead, He says, "Pray, and don't lose heart." This is because Jesus' story is not just about prayer. It's about how prayer affects our deep questions about social injustice.

The first character in the story is a judge. He works in a city, probably in a civil court, but he's not exactly a model citizen (see Luke 18:2). In fact, he's as corrupt as they come: He "did not fear God and did not respect man," Jesus tells us (v. 2, NASB). This is a highly unfavorable description from Jesus, who taught that the two greatest commandments were to love God and love your neighbor (Matthew 22:36–40).

When somebody in a position of authority not only doesn't have reverence for God but doesn't even have respect for other people, injustice and abuse are sure to follow. That's exactly what the second character has to face. She is a widow who wants to bring her case to court.

To Jesus' original audience, the mention of a widow would have immediately signified not just a person who had lost her husband, but a symbol of everyone who needs help and compassion. Throughout the Scriptures, God commands us to treat widows charitably and threatens severe judgment on those who neglect them. "Ye shall not afflict any widow, or fatherless child" commands the Torah (Exodus 22:22, KJV). In the New Testament, James describes "pure religion" as the kind that "visit[s] the fatherless and widows in their affliction" (James 1:27, KJV). God cares for—and wants us to care for—everyone who is vulnerable, needy, and alone.

This widow has a problem: someone has been trying to illegally take advantage of her. As a widow, she doesn't have the power or the resources she needs to protect herself. But the law is clearly on her side. She knows that if only she can get her case to court, she'll receive legal protection from her opponent. The law and the evidence are in her favor. Now she just needs some justice.

Unfortunately, as long as that judge is on the bench, that's exactly what she can't get. As we might have expected from his introduction, the corrupt judge completely ignored the widow's requests. The representative of justice is unjust.

The widow is now oppressed on two sides: her opponent is harassing her, and the figure of authority doesn't care. It looks hopeless. This is when many people would start to feel demoralized and alone, questioning whether God is on their side.

But the widow has a character trait that serves her well: persistence. Jesus tells us that she "kept coming" (Luke 18:3, NASB). In Greek, the verb is in what's known as the "imperfect middle," which indicates that the action is continually repeated. Even when she might have been discouraged, she just didn't quit. Every spare moment she had, she was going back to the judge, pestering him, bothering him, annoying him, and asking him the same thing over and over and over again. He ignored her every time. She kept asking. He ignored her again. She asked again. He ignored her some more. She asked some more.

2. THE WIDOW WON'T GIVE UP (vv. 4–6)

Finally, the judge had enough. Jesus describes his thoughts like this: "Even though I do not fear God nor respect man, yet because this widow bothers me, I will give her legal protection, otherwise by continually coming she will wear me out" (Luke 18:4–5, NASB). The words translated "wear me out" are literally "hit me in the eye." This is not a threat of physical violence but a vivid metaphor for something that is so continually annoying you can't stand it anymore. The widow's persistence sent the message that she wouldn't give up until she got what she needed. Eventually, her unrelenting pleas for justice annoyed the judge so much that he gave in.

The judge didn't really have a change of heart. He didn't mend his ways and begin to respect God or his neighbors. The laws didn't change, society wasn't restructured, and nobody stepped in and revolutionized anything. What brought about the result the widow needed was nothing more than her plain and simple persistence.

What's the lesson Jesus wants us to learn from His story? At first, it seems obvious enough. "Hear what the unrighteous judge said," He says (v. 6, NASB). That much is clear:

persistence pays off! Even when there is no other change, as long as we keep on asking for the justice and fair treatment we need, eventually we will find it.

3. THE EXPLANATION (vv. 7–9)

Is it really that simple? Is this just a little fable to tell us the shopworn moral of "Try, try again"? We might be tempted to think that until Jesus continues His explanation:

> *Now, will not God bring about justice for His elect who cry to Him day and night, and will He delay long over them? I tell you that He will bring about justice for them quickly. However, when the Son of Man comes, will He find faith on the earth? (vv. 7–8, NASB)*

This is much less comfortable. Why does Jesus make an analogy between the unjust judge and God? Is it really fair to say that God "will bring about justice for them quickly" when so many prayers seem to go unanswered for years? And what's up with that last question about whether faith will be found on the earth?

The purpose of Jesus' analogy is probably the easiest to understand. Jesus takes it for granted that His Father is completely unlike the unjust judge in His attitude to people. But if that's the case, why does Jesus draw a parallel between God and the unjust judge?

The key is found in what's called *a fortiori* argument, a Latin phrase that means "from the stronger." The argument takes this form: "If this fact is true in this case, think how much more strongly it must be true in a better case!" Unlike the unjust judge, God cares for widows and others in need. God is loving, kind, compassionate, merciful, and eager to see justice done. God responds to His people's prayers.

As the unrighteous judge shows us, persistence is essential for bringing about justice. The *a fortiori* argument applies this to God: If continual, persistent demands can bring about justice when we ask an unsympathetic, unjust human judge, imagine what it can accomplish when we ask our Father who is sympathetic, caring, and passionate about justice!

However, there is one particular area where God does seem to be like the unjust judge. It can take Him a long time to answer our prayers. If God is really so eager to bring us justice, then what reason does He have for waiting to answer our prayers—sometimes for months, sometimes years, sometimes generations? Why doesn't He always give us such a good thing right away?

Logically, we have only two options: Either God is not as good as Jesus makes Him out to be, or He has an even better reason for waiting to give us what we ask for. Which one we choose to believe will depend on where we look. We can look at the suffering and injustice around us, be discouraged, and give up on God. Many people have abandoned their faith for precisely this reason. Or we can look at Jesus' words and trust Him when He says, *"I tell you that He will bring about justice for them quickly"* (v. 7, emphasis added).

Which should we trust: circumstances of injustice we can see, or a promise of justice we haven't seen yet? That depends on what kind of person is making the promise. If it's someone we don't know, we have no reason to trust their promise. But the better we know someone, the more we know how much we can trust them. If we know someone well enough to know that they will keep their word, we can trust them however long it seems to take.

That's where prayer comes in. It's a cliché to say "prayer is communication with God," but the only way to get to know someone is to communicate with them. If we took our requests to God only once and He immediately answered them, we would never have the chance to get to know Him in any meaningful way. We would not have a heavenly Father but a fairy godmother.

Instead, God arranges things so that we can come to Him persistently. We can bring Him our requests, our concerns, our fears, our feelings of injustice, our anger, our frustration, our grief, our joy. But we don't bring these requests and feelings to Him the way the widow brought them to the unjust judge. With God, our worries fall on sympathetic ears.

Persistence in prayer—praying for the same things repeatedly—does not show a lack of faith. Jesus Himself prayed multiple times for the same request (see Matthew 26:44), which surely didn't show any deficiency on His part. Rather, persistence in the face of trials produces a godly character that enables us to have hope. Paul explained:

> Not only so, but we also rejoice in our sufferings, because we know that suffering produces perseverance; perseverance, character; and character, hope. And hope does not disappoint us, because God has poured out his love into our hearts by the Holy Spirit, whom he has given us (Romans 5:3–5, NIV).

Evangelist and Bible scholar R. A. Torrey eloquently summed up this aspect of the parable:

> The exact force of the parable is that if even an unrighteous judge will yield to persistent prayer and grant the thing that he did not wish to grant, how much more will a loving God yield to the persistent cries of His children and give the things that He longs to give, but which it would not be wise to give, would not be for their own good, unless they were trained to that persevering faith that will not take no for an answer....Why is it that God does not give to us the things that we ask, the first time we ask? The answer is plain: He would do us the far greater good of training us in persistent faith. (Torrey, "Keep Praying Until God Answers")

While it's true that persistence is essential to faith, we must beware of imagining God sitting up in heaven holding off on dispensing justice until we have prayed long enough to impress Him. This false picture is demolished by God's real response to suffering. In the person of Jesus Christ, God Himself came down to earth and experienced what it was to be rejected, oppressed, betrayed, falsely accused, and executed on false charges. On the Cross, Jesus bore not only our sins but also our griefs and sorrows (see Isaiah 53:4).

Just as He was in the fiery furnace with Shadrach, Meshach, and Abednego, Jesus is present with us when we suffer (Daniel 3:24–25). God took our suffering and made it His own. Receiving social justice and equality would be hollow if we had no one to love us, support us, and accept us. Even more than we need justice, we need love. By suffering with us, God shows His love for us and gives us an unchangeable reason to trust in His goodness.

When we know God, we will know peace, security, and consolation even in the face of suffering and oppression. As Paul exhorted elsewhere, "Do not be anxious about anything, but in everything, by prayer and petition, with thanksgiving, present your requests to God. And the peace of God, which transcends all understanding, will guard your hearts and your minds in Christ Jesus" (Philippians 4:6–7, NIV).

That doesn't mean that God doesn't care whether we receive justice. Far from it—the better we know Him, the more certain we will be that He wants to do everything He can to bring about justice for us. God's character gives us a foundation for hope even when we cannot see the results of our prayers or efforts.

This explains Jesus' closing remarks: "I tell you that He will bring about justice for them quickly. However, when the Son of Man comes, will He find faith on the earth?" (Luke 18:8, NASB). Jesus is certain that God will bring about justice, but He leaves it an open question as to whether we will have faith. Justice is up to God, but do we trust Him?

Jesus knows the coming years will cause us to doubt God's goodness. Suffering and oppression will devastate and shake our logical certainties. Even Jesus Himself, during His time of greatest suffering, prayed, "MY GOD, MY GOD, WHY HAVE YOU FORSAKEN ME?" (Mark 15:34, NASB). It is not a question of whether we will feel pain, rejection, and abandonment. Of course we will. The question is whether we will still pray, "*My* God."

Our prayers are not what cause God to give justice. Prayer brings us close to God, which causes us to have faith that He will give justice even when we don't see it. Because of Jesus' own anguish, we can pray without giving up because we know that God knows what it is to suffer. Because of our persistent prayers, we can work for justice without giving up. We can have faith that God is on the side of justice. However long it takes, we can pray at all times and never give up.

REFLECTIONS ⌐

1. *Do you see God as just or unjust? Why? How does this parable affect or change the way you think about God?*
2. *How would you answer Jesus' question: "When the Son of man comes, will He find faith on the earth?"*
3. *What are some things that might cause you to lose heart in praying or seeking justice? How can you keep from being discouraged or giving up?*

DECIDING MY RESPONSIBILITY ⌐

PERSONAL
Have you ever been angry with God because of unanswered prayers? Have you stopped praying, lost heart, or given up? How does this parable affect your feelings about God? What needs to change for you to pray more persistently?

COMMUNITY
Can you identify any situations in your community that are unfair toward disadvantaged people? If so, what can you do to help everyone receive the fair treatment God wants them to have? Develop a plan for persistent prayer and action, and keep it up until you see good results.

CLOSING PRAYER ⌐

Lord, we thank You that You are not an unjust judge but the Judge of all the earth who will surely do what is right. We believe that You are faithful to keep all Your promises, and we trust You to bring about justice as You have promised for everyone. But even more than You want us to be treated fairly, You want us to know You, trust You, and love You. We thank You that You are a great High Priest who understands our suffering because You suffer with us.

Help us to persistently seek You in prayer so that we can know Your love and extend that love to our neighbors. In Jesus' name we pray. Amen.

SOURCES

"Memorable Quotes for *Fiddler on the Roof (1971).*" *Internet Movie Database.* http://www.imdb.com/title/tt0067093/quotes (accessed July 5, 2010).

"Persisting." *Merriam-Webster Online Dictionary.* Merriam-Webster Online. http://www.merriam-webster.com/dictionary/persisting (accessed July 7, 2010).

Blue Letter Bible. "Gospel of Luke 18 (King James Version)." Blue Letter Bible. 1996–2010. http://www.blueletterbible.org/Bible.cfm?b=Luk&c=18&t=KJV (accessed July 7, 2010).

Torrey, R. A. "Keep Praying Until God Answers." The R. A. Torrey Archive. http://ratorrey.webs.com/Keep%20Praying%20Until%20God%20Answers.htm (accessed June 5, 2010).

——. "Widows." In *Torrey's New Topical Textbook.* http://www.ccel.org/ccel/torrey/ttt.html?term=Widows (accessed June 10, 2010).

10

THE PHARISEE AND THE TAX COLLECTOR

Based on Luke 18:9–14

KEY VERSE ⁓

"NOT BY WORKS OF RIGHTEOUSNESS
WHICH WE HAVE DONE, BUT
ACCORDING TO HIS MERCY HE SAVED
US, BY THE WASHING OF REGENERATION,
AND RENEWING OF THE HOLY GHOST"

(Titus 3:5, KJV).

OPENING PRAYER ⁓

*Lord, thank You for your mercy, which is available to
us even when we have doubts about tomorrow. Help us
Lord to humble ourselves before You, recognizing You
as the Author and Finisher of our faith, the only hope
of salvation. Amen.*

WORDS TO CONSIDER ⁓

1. **JUSTIFIED (Luke 18:14).** To be deemed free from any
punishment.
2. **MERCIFUL (v. 13).** Showing God's clemency or forgiveness for any sin or affront to Him.
3. **PHARISEE (vv. 10, 11).** A member of the ruling class of
religious leaders.
4. **PUBLICAN (vv. 10, 11, 13).** A tax collector.
5. **TEMPLE (v. 10).** The center of Hebrew worship in Jerusalem.
6. **TORAH. (v. 10, Exposition).** Law.

INTRODUCTION ⁓

The parable that Jesus set forth in Luke 18:9–14 confronts a common question: Won't my good works get me to heaven? While the answer may seem obvious to us, the question is asked in subtle and profound ways through popular culture and in the church. Consider the song "Change Gone Come" written by Sam Cooke ("Sam Cooke," Answers.com). It echoes this question in the line: "It's been too hard living, but I'm afraid to die, 'cause I don't know what's up there beyond the sky." This line sums up the dilemma of all who struggle in this life and find themselves wondering about life after death. It can be a cry of anguish or a plea for divine grace. As you approach this study of Jesus' parable of the Pharisee and the publican, do so with fresh eyes knowing that this dilemma has been faced by all who hunger and thirst after righteousness—even when they think they know the answer.

SCRIPTURE TEXT —

> **LUKE 18:9, KJV** *And he spake this parable unto certain which trusted in themselves that they were righteous, and despised others:* **10** *Two men went up into the temple to pray; the one a Pharisee, and the other a publican.* **11** *The Pharisee stood and prayed thus with himself, God, I thank thee, that I am not as other men are, extortioners, unjust, adulterers, or even as this publican.* **12** *I fast twice in the week, I give tithes of all that I possess.* **13** *And the publican, standing afar off, would not lift up so much as his eyes unto heaven, but smote upon his breast, saying, God be merciful to me a sinner.* **14** *I tell you, this man went down to his house justified rather than the other: for every one that exalteth himself shall be abased; and he that humbleth himself shall be exalted.*

BIBLE BACKGROUND —

Luke is the only Gospel writer to include this parable. Perhaps this is because Luke was not a Jew. Luke was well aware that he fit the description Paul put forth in Ephesians 2:12, which describes converted Gentiles as once being "without Christ, being aliens from the commonwealth of Israel, and strangers from the covenants of promise, having no hope, and without God in the world." As a Gentile, Luke appreciated that our salvation lies only in God's mercy and grace.

The parable of the Pharisee and the publican was told by Jesus to a Jewish audience, yet it fit perfectly with the Greek audience of Luke's day, "a culture that glorified wisdom, beauty, and the ideal man" (Jensen, 1977). The power of this parable must have held special value to Luke as it would to his friend, Theophilus (Luke 1:3), and the Greek audiences to whom this Gospel was surely circulated.

EXPLORING THE MEANING ⌐

1. THE PROBLEM (LUKE 18:9)

Lesson 10 examines the second parable in Luke 18 and the final parable in our 10-session Bible study. The parable in Luke 18:9–14 begins with a declaration that while the parable was spoken to everyone, it was directed to those who proudly consider themselves to be righteous by their own actions and attitudes. This parable was directed at those who "trust" (Gk. *peitho*, **PI-tho**) in themselves. The New International Version says, "confident of their own righteousness" (18:9). This particular concept of "being righteous" (Gk. *dikaios*, **dik-AH-yo-sis**) refers to "self-imposed rules" by a person who "having set up and kept or pretended to keep, certain standards, they called themselves righteous or just in the sight of God." In reality, these acts are merely a "performance of external ceremonial ordinances" (Zodhiates, 1985).

Such self-righteous attitudes alone are condemning, but Jesus went further in denouncing these behaviors. The sin of self-righteousness is compounded because this attitude also "despised" (Gk. *exoutheneo*, **ex-oo-then-EH-oo**) others, counting them as worthless and useless vagrants before God. The sin then is twofold: disrespect for God's call to righteousness through a contrite heart toward Him, and disregard for fellow humans for whom God has concern.

2. THE PEOPLE AND THE PLACE (v. 10)

In verse 10, Jesus sets the scene for this interesting comparison of two men. Both were in the same situation and place. They were Jews going to the Temple to pray. Jesus also relates that these men represented two extremes in the religious world, because one was a Pharisee and the other a publican.

The first man was a Pharisee. The Pharisee represents those held in the highest regard for their piety and allegiance to the Law. The Pharisees and Sadducees were the political ruling classes of Jewish culture and religion. The Pharisees called for strict adherence to minute details of the Torah. Their interpretation of the Law demanded adherence to the traditions. Less wealthy than the Sadducees, the Pharisees were more influential among the people. Even though the Pharisees were considered laity, not priests, they held the seat of the high priest in the Sanhedrin, the highest court of Jewish civil and religious authority at the time of Jesus' ministry. The Pharisees vehemently opposed Jesus because he did not obey their laws or match their concept of how God would reveal the Messiah (*NIV Archaeological Study Bible*, 2005).

The second man was a publican or tax collector. He represents those who were most likely to be cheating scoundrels whose allegiance was to their personal wealth rather than to God. Their reputation was earned because they levied and collected Roman taxes and often took bribes. For this reason, they were considered traitors to the Jewish community.

For first century Jews, the temple at Jerusalem was the center of worship. This was the temple of Herod. It was built by the Roman government to resemble the plan of Solomon's temple, the grand and stationery replacement for the tabernacle where Israel worshiped in the Wilderness. While synagogues were located throughout Israel as places of prayer and Torah study, the temple, with its focus on the system of sacrifices given to Moses in the Wilderness, represented the central location for worshiping God. It was not at all unusual that both men went to the temple. Jews, male and female, of all social backgrounds, as well as proselytes or converts to Judaism, all went to the temple. Their seating within the structure varied, but all who wanted to pray to the God of Israel went to the temple to do so. These two men, however, were in the same area of the temple because they were both Jewish males.

3. THE PROUD PROCLAMATION (vv. 11–12)
Even though the Pharisee begins his prayer with "God," he prays to himself as he offers thanks to God for his good points and everyone else's failures! He starts with thankfulness that he is not like other men, whom he generously names: "extortioners, unjust, adulterers, or even as this publican" (18:11). It seems that in each description, he is comparing himself to the publican.

"Extortioners" was probably a fitting stereotypical description for publicans because of their reputation for shamelessly taking money from the poor to feed Roman coffers and their own pockets. "Unjust" is a reference to those who are without faith and who fall short in righteousness. Again, this indicates not only those who are not followers of the Law to the letter, but also those who, like the majority of the publicans, are so greedy that they take what belongs to others, failing to honor God in their actions.

The reference to an adulterer could have a double meaning. First, the reference is to those who are unfaithful to a spouse. Abstaining from adultery is one of the Ten Commandments (Exodus 20:14). But adultery means more than the abuse of the marital relationship. It is also a symbolic abuse of the love of God for His people. Israel was often called adulterous for neglecting their obligation to God. The attitudes of publicans showed allegiance to money and Rome rather than to God. All of these references seem to point to the publican, who in the end is named by the Pharisee.

After lambasting the publican and publicly listing all of the publican's assumed faults as non-descriptors of his own righteousness, the Pharisee names his own good points, the first of which is habitual fasting. Old Testament fasting was required by Law only on the Day of Atonement (Leviticus 16:29–31). At other times, fasting was a voluntary declaration of either a communal concern or a personal one. Following the Jewish exile in 582 B.C., additional fast days became common. During the New Testament period, fasting was still practiced, and the Pharisees created a ritual around it. They fasted twice weekly—Mondays and Thursdays (*NIV Archaeological Study Bible*, 2005).

Jesus participated in and understood fasting (Matthew 4:2; 9:14–15). The issue with this Pharisee, therefore, was not that he fasted, but that he boasted about it and counted it as a righteous act that would gain him special favor with God. This Pharisee probably went to great lengths on Mondays and Thursdays to look like he was fasting (Matthew 6:16). But it seems unnecessary that he should announce his fasts in his prayer, since fasting should be directed "only to your Father, who is unseen, and your Father, who sees what is done in secret, will reward you" (Matthew 6:18, NIV). It is obvious then that the man was boasting not just to God, but to everyone who could hear him (*NIV Archaeological Study Bible*, 2005).

The second self-righteous act the Pharisee mentioned was that he gave a tithe of all he possessed. The Pharisee was clearly not poor. In fact, he was so rich that his righteous act, in contrast to an extortioner, was that he paid a tithe on all he had. He didn't cheat God in his tithe.

4. THE PITIFUL CRY (vv. 13–14)

At this point, both the Pharisee and the publican stood. The Pharisee "stood and prayed," probably in a prominent spot at the front of the temple area. Although he was on his feet, the publican was humbled to the point of shamefully averting his gaze from the heavens and from anyone who happened to be near his "afar off" place (18:13).

The usual posture for prayer was standing with "eyes and hands lifted to heaven." This was probably the Pharisee's posture. The publican, however, repeatedly "beat" (Gr. *tupto,* **TOOP-to**) upon his chest. This is a gesture of remorse and mourning for sin against God. The gesture was usually coupled with some act of restitution. There is no mention that the publican brought such an offering or even made a promise to make amends to God. Not doing so condemned him even more in the sight of those who were accustomed to the Pharisaic prayers of the day (*IVP Bible Background Commentary,* 1993).

Notice that the publican also began his prayer by calling on God, but he uttered only a single sentence—a plea for mercy. The term used for "mercy" (Gk. *hilaskomai,* **hil-AS-kom-ahee**) means to make restitution. The publican knew he was unworthy and knew that he could not pay God to make up for his basic lack. In essence, the publican was declaring that he was unworthy to bring any gift of restitution. He needed the intervention of God to forgive his sins and transgressions. The publican was asking that God's mercy provide "the satisfaction demanded by God's justice" and replace the punishment of sin with peace between the publican and God (Zodhiates, 1985).

At this point, Jesus gives the final analysis of this parable. Jesus' statement takes this parable from the setting in the temple to a place of judgment before God. In essence, these two men have come to the temple to make their pleas before God in hopes that God will accept them. Jesus' response is a proclamation of judgment.

This is a shift in how first century Jews (and perhaps we, too) view prayer. The Pharisee's prayer seems boastfulness to us, but it may not have seemed that way to its first century audience. *The IVP Bible Background Commentary* warns that the first hearers of this parable would not have thought the Pharisee to be self-righteous. They would simply have thought it honorable that the Pharisee was grateful to God for his righteousness (Keener, 1993). It was shocking, then, to hear Jesus say that the publican, rather than the Pharisee, was justified before God.

"Justification" (Gk. *dikaiosis,* **dik-AH-yo-sis**) means to be free from the punishment of God for sin. The *Hebrew-Greek Key Study Bible* points out that the verb tense "generally means to bring out that which is or that which is desired" (Zodhiates, 1985). In this case, the recognition of righteousness before God is brought out or revealed in these two men. To be "righteous" (Gk. *dikaios,* **dik-AH-yos**) before God is to be "right," to be seen as having not committed any sins or transgressions. Neither righteousness nor justification can be achieved by human means. (See Romans 3:10, 23.)

Jesus' explanation, then, is that the publican pled his case by falling on the mercy of God's court. The publican looked to God for a means of justification, realizing that nothing in his power or being was worthy to stand before God. Because the Pharisee exalted himself, he will be humbled at the judgment of God. Likewise, anyone who publicly or privately in their hearts makes proud and haughty declarations about following God and doing "the right thing" will have to replace such attitudes with humility. Only by being humble before God will we be exalted.

CONCLUSION

We began this study with the question, "Won't my good works get me to heaven?" John Bunyan's *Pilgrim's Progress* confronts this question head-on in the allegorical tale of Christian, a man who undertakes a journey toward salvation. When asked by the character, Evangelist, why he has chosen to do this quest, Christian responds, "I perceive by the Book in my hand, that I am condemned to die, and after that to come to Judgment, and I find that I am not willing to do the first, nor able to do the second." Whether we relate our own doubts to the questions in the journey of Christians or the words of Sam Cooke's "Change Gone Come," we can rest assured that God heard our cry. He opened the door to salvation through the sacrifice paid by Jesus Christ, knowing that only in Him can we be justified before God.

REFLECTIONS

1. *Think about the act of prayer as a plea to God. In what ways have you entered prayer by thanking God for what you have or have not done? In your next time of devotion, alter your prayer by asking for God's mercy and confessing why you're in need of His grace.*

2. *Consider the references this lesson has made to* Pilgrim's Progress *and "Change Gone Come." Identify times when those or similar thoughts about life and heaven have made you doubt or brought you to humbly seek God's help. How did you feel? How did you approach God? How did God respond? What in that experience can help you seek God's grace now?*

3. *The Pharisee said he gave all he had to the poor. Reflect on your faithfulness to tithing your income or donating financially to God's work. Are you doing all you can, or are you holding back resources? More importantly, what is your motive for giving? Are you giving out of love for God and your neighbors or out of a desire to impress people?*

4. *This parable opened with Jesus saying that those who are self-righteous look down on others. Think about your attitude toward homeless people, those who beg on the street, and those whose apparel seems inappropriate or culturally misguided. How do you feel about them? Does your attitude reveal any self-righteousness? How?*

5. *Reread the key verse for this lesson (Titus 3:5). Why do you think this verse was selected as a key verse? What light does it shed on this study?*

DECIDING MY RESPONSIBILITY

PERSONAL

1. *Do you have children or are you responsible for mentoring and encouraging someone who is new to the faith? Share this parable with them as a way of discussing how we can recognize attitudes that are haughty rather than humble.*

2. *"Pharisee bashing" is easy in this text; however, that is a strategy for self-justification also. After all, when we condemn the Pharisee, don't we look good? Rewrite the Pharisee's prayer in a way that shows a humble spirit. Then reflect on whether the rewritten prayer helps you see what true humility is.*

COMMUNITY

Many churches feed the hungry or give clothing away. If we are not careful, these acts of kindness can become acts of self-righteousness where we perform a duty "to those less fortunate." In your next ministry meeting, brainstorm how you can humbly touch human lives while doing outreach ministry. Here are a few starter questions:

1. Do workers talk to each other more than to those being served? When they speak to those being served, is it a conversation or just instructions?
2. Would you eat the food you serve in outreach settings as it is presented?
3. Are you doing what is needed? Food and clothing may be an issue, but could those efforts be coupled with other ministries? Brainstorm how you could enhance the existing ministry with one-on-one counseling, one-on-one prayer, homework help for children, or other services.

CLOSING PRAYER ⌣

Father, Thank You for the revelation of what pleases and honors You. Help us to be humble in Your presence and in what we do in honoring Your name. Amen.

SOURCES

"Cooke, Sam." Answers.com. http://www.answers.com/topic/sam-cooke (accessed June 20, 2010).

"Fasting in the Bible and the Ancient Near East." *NIV Archaeological Study Bible.* Grand Rapids, MI: Zondervan, 2005. 1568.

Jensen, Irving. *Jensen's Survey of the New Testament.* Chicago: Moody Press, 1977. 159.

Keener, Craig S. *The IVP Bible Background Commentary.* Downers Grove, IL: InterVarsity Press, 1993. 239.

"The Pharisees." *NIV Archaeological Study Bible.* Grand Rapids, MI: Zondervan, 2005. 1566.

"Prominent Jewish Religious Groups." *Life Application Study Bible.* Wheaton, IL: Tyndale House of Publishers, 1991. 1731.

"The Sanhedrin." *NIV Archaeological Study Bible.* Grand Rapids, MI: Zondervan, 2005. 1821.

Zodhiates, Spiros. *Hebrew-Greek Key Study Bible.* Chattanooga, TN: AMG Publishers, 1985. 1681, 1698, 1720.

NOTES

NOTES

NOTES

NOTES